When It Was Yet Dark

James Howard Trott

The first day of the week cometh Mary Magdalene early, when it was yet dark, unto the sepulchre, and seeth the stone taken away from the sepulchre. – John 20:1

Oak and Yew Press

When It Was Yet Dark

James Howard Trott

Oak and Yew Press

OAK AND YEW
PRESS

Mary Magdalene at the tomb, from a Bible card, artist unknown, ca 1927.

Heaviness May Endure for a Night, But Joy Cometh in the Morning

Christina Rossetti

No thing is great on this side of the grave,
Nor any thing of any stable worth:
Whatso is born from earth returns to earth:
No thing we grasp proves half the thing we crave:
The tidal wave shrinks to the ebbing wave:
Laughter is folly, madness lurks in mirth:
Mankind sets off a-dying from the birth:
Life is a losing game, with what to save?
Thus I sat mourning like a mournful owl,
And like a doleful dragon made ado,
Companion of all monsters of the dark:
When lo the light cast off its nightly cowl,
And up to heaven flashed a carolling lark.
And all creation sang its hymn anew.

While all creation sang its hymn anew
What could I do but sing a stave in tune?
Spectral on high hung pale the vanishing moon
Where a last gleam of stars hung paling too.
Lark's lay--a cockcrow--with a scattered few
Soft early chirpings--with a tender croon
Of doves--a hundred thousand calls, and soon
A hundred thousand answers sweet and true.
These set me singing too at unawares:
One note for all delights and charities,
One note for hope reviving with the light,
One note for every lovely thing that is;
Till while I sang my heart shook off its cares
And revelled in the land of no more night.

CONTENTS

Frontispiece – Mary Magdalene at the tomb

Poem - *Heaviness May Endure for a Night, But Joy Cometh in the Morning* by Christina Rossetti

BIBLE VERSION: All scripture passages are given at the beginning of each chapter in the King James version.

PASSAGES: The four sections of the gospels which are central to our reflections here are: Matthew 27:1-10; 27:50-28:20 [end]; Mark 15:37- 16:20 [end]; Luke 23:46-24:53 [end]; John 19:30-21:25 [end].

CHAPTERS: Each chapter of this work is a brief exposition of the primary passages. Each one focuses on particular persons and events. Beyond this, each chapter deals with central themes, and then some parallel teaching in related passages.

When It Was Yet Dark

Some of the more intriguing passages of the four gospels are found in the last few chapters of each. Especially germane to our struggles of faith are those accounts of the period between the death and resurrection of the Lord. As we ask ourselves how we can "keep on keeping on," we are talking about the great "mystery of godliness" (I Timothy 3:16): Christ "believed on in the world". Part of our answer may be found in the continued faithfulness, even the renewed and *heightened* faithfulness of many of Jesus' followers during this time when there was no evident basis for it.

Following Jesus' death his disciples and followers (apparently without exception) were convinced he had failed and their hopes were come to an end. Why then did they continue to devote themselves to such things as preparing his body for burial? Why did they continue to gather together? Why did they continue to identify themselves with him, when the chances of continuing retribution and persecution were high and no rewards were conceivable? The answers to these questions are significant for us as we struggle to persevere.

The biggest battles of the Christian life take place "when it is yet dark" -- when things are unclear or appear hopeless. This book is centrally focused on faith in times when the evidence dictates despair. I would not like anyone to mistake this book for a "self-help manual," however.

Books which focus on the "self" are often contradictory and even "self-hindering". The same can be true of "counseling," or "therapy" or even "spiritual healing" ministry to the degree that it is oriented around "self": "self-knowledge", "self-realization," et cetera, or even solely focused upon ones own faith and sanctification. When Jay Adams published his landmark book *Competent to Counsel* in the 1960's, it was definitely and deliberately a revolutionary document. The revolution was against the prevailing doctrines of psychology which were assailing the church. Adams reminded the church that God was equipping every believer for teaching, exhorting, encouraging and rebuking each other by means of the scriptures through the power of the Holy Spirit. His stated purpose was to encourage every churchman to pick up his Bible and apply it first to himself, then to his brother.

However, Christians are always in danger of unwittingly absorbing the radically individual, "self"-centered orientation of the world and secular psychology. As we encourage one another as "competent to counsel" it is important we affirm the more fundamental and universal power of scripture to right what is wrong in the context of the church. The power is not in the preacher but in the text applied to our hearts by the Holy Spirit and applied to one another daily. The power is in the scriptures lived out together. And I must add, the power is not in the words of the Christian writer, but in the Word of God, sharp and active for "one-anothering" through encouragement, warning, teaching, and exhorting.

This then is a Bible study, a series of meditations with a few mini-sermons looming out of it here and there. In these passages of scripture we see the lives of the first Christians transformed. In increased reliance on the word of God our lives are being similarly transformed together.

There are a number of persons who stand out in the gospel narratives covering the period from the crucifixion to the ascension. These include: the independent witnesses (the centurion and crowd at the crucifixion), the faithful women (together with John), Joseph of Arimathea, Nicodemus, Judas, Mary Magdalene (again), Peter and John, Thomas, the two on the road to Emmaus, and the Galilean "fishing caucus".

SECTION I : WHEN IT WAS YET DARK

From the Crucifixion
to the Revealing of the Resurrection

Chapter One: Independent Witnesses

-- The centurion et al

Matthew 27:50-54
50 Jesus, when he had cried again with a loud voice, yielded up the ghost
51 And, behold, the veil of the temple was rent in twain from the top to the bottom; and the earth did quake, and the rocks rent;
[52 And the graves were opened, and many bodies of the saints which slept arose,
53 and came out of the graves after his resurrection, and went into the holy city, and appeared unto many.]
54 Now when the centurion, and they that were with him, watching Jesus, saw the earthquake, and those things that were done, they feared greatly, saying, Truly this was the Son of God.

Mark 15:37-39
37 And Jesus cried with a loud voice, and gave up the ghost.
38 And the veil of the temple was rent in twain from the top to the bottom.
39 And when the centurion, which stood over against him, saw that he so cried out, and gave up the ghost, he said, Truly this man was the Son of God.

Luke 23:44b-48
44b ...and there was darkness over all the earth until the ninth hour.

3.

45 And the sun was darkened, and the veil of the temple was rent in the midst.
46 and when Jesus had cried with a loud voice, he said, Father into thy hands I commend my spirit: and having said thus, he gave up the ghost.
47 Now when the centurion saw what was done, he glorified God, saying, Certainly this was a righteous man.
48 And all the people that came together to that sight, beholding the things which were done, smote their breasts, and returned.

To the onlookers, the final "events" of Christ's crucifixion raised the drama from a pathetic to an epic level. The chief witnesses at this point are not the church, which is scattered, skulking, and with only a few representatives present. These witnesses are mostly curious bystanders, not comprehending what goes on in terms of biblical-theological significance. Rather they have thus far watched it as a not unfamiliar juridical and political event.

It is a familiar event because they often saw the standard Roman form of capital punishment being carried out -- this time on three criminals. It is unfamiliar insofar as most of the crowd have heard that Jesus is not a run-of-the-mill criminal. Some of them have heard him preach and seen him work wonders. Most of them have heard about his claims and the accusations against him. All of them know that there is a strong political element to the execution. A few suspect this man is being added to the long list of Israel's persecuted prophets. But with all these variations, they are basically a crowd come together as crowds have gathered at executions down through the centuries.

Many commentators on these passages nevertheless emphasize the importance of these and subsequent witnesses. The Christian faith is firmly founded on the resurrection, as Paul says, "If Christ be not raised we are of all men most foolish". Therefore it is God's plan and mercy that we are furnished with so many different kinds of eye-witnesses and accounts to this most important series of events.

The first on record is a centurion (some traditions would even make him the same centurion of whom Jesus said, "I have not seen such faith, no not in all of Israel") who seems to be on duty at the execution. We see that this centurion is right beside Jesus (Mark 15:39) and that he is not alone in witnessing the final events (Matthew 27:54). He seems to be the officer in charge of the execution detail. He is the one Pilate sends for later to determine if Jesus is dead, after Joseph of Arimathaea asks for the body.

As Jesus dies, the centurion states his verdict: that Jesus was truly the Son of God and a righteous man (compare Matthew and Mark with Luke on this). What is it that he witnesses, along with his cohort, and the crowd, many of whom conclude likewise? (Luke 23:47-8) It does not appear that Jesus' facial expression, or his early words of charity and suffering, or even his final words are the primary factor in the conclusion reached by these witnesses. Rather it is these things in conjunction with the unusual, even cataclysmic things going on.

After Jesus cried out in a loud voice," Eli, eli, lama sabacthani," he cries out again with a loud voice (this is the only time we are not given the words he speaks from the cross -- so we incline to conclude he cried out in an unintelligible voice.) He then says, "Father into thy hands I commend my spirit," and dies. Mark seems to emphasize these last words and cry as the basis for the centurion's conclusions. Matthew and Luke, however, emphasize that it was "the things done" in conjunction with these last cries that convinced the witnesses of Jesus' righteous and divine status. And what were these things? Nothing Jesus did, certainly, for we are told of nothing he did except speak, and refuse to drink. He certainly did not take the advice of those who mocked him -- neither coming down from the cross, or otherwise saving them and himself, nor doing any other sign equivalent to those many wonders of healing and provision he had done among them previously.

"The things done" seem to have been done on a larger scale than most of Jesus' miracles hitherto. We are told, first, that the sky had been growing dark for at least three hours; that the sun itself is blotted out at this climactic moment; that the earth is shaken with an earthquake so that the rocks were "rent," that is torn, perhaps with fissures opening up in the very vicinity of Golgotha; and that other very frightening things were happening, many of which must have been evident to those gathered there. The chronology of the narrative requires us to pay close attention -- especially in Matthew, where we read that the tombs opened up and the dead came forth -- but then we are told that this was after Jesus rose. (Matthew rushes ahead in recounting these things in the same breath, so to speak, because he has come to see these events as all of a piece -- Jesus' death and his resurrection and the wonders that accompanied both.)

The veil of the Temple was torn in two, top to bottom, but no one at the Place of the Skull could have known this at the time. It seems, then, it was the manner of Jesus' dying, and in particular his words of faith, in combination with the literally earth-shaking catastrophes of terrain and atmosphere which convinced the witnesses.

It is tempting to attribute more theological insight to these witnesses than the account warrants. If the centurion was indeed that one whom Jesus earlier commended, then he was educated in the faith of Israel, and had a further basis for understanding that Jesus was indeed Messiah and Savior, because Jesus had healed his servant. Certainly few others understood this, and it's unlikely that this centurion did either -- that he was not the one earlier commended by Jesus, but rather was merely interpreting these cataclysms within his own pagan world view as the kinds of things that would have happened if a hero (the mortal child of a god) had died. His use of the term "Son of God" may not indicate an affirmation of Jesus true status. Nonetheless, it is certainly an affirmation that he is someone special, and the events surrounding his death unique.

The place of the crowd in the crucifixion narratives is like that of the chorus in many Greek plays, or various minor characters in English-language drama. They see what transpires and reinforce the observations of those hearing or seeing the story. They do very little interpretation. What they say only confirms what is most significant to this audience, yet it crystallizes and makes explicit things we might not have explicitly formulated ourselves. Like the guards at the beginning of *Hamlet*, the centurion and the crowd think they have seen a powerful supernatural manifestation, but wiser witnesses with more intimate knowledge are needed to make clear what has happened.

When all is said and done, these accounts show us that Jesus was recognized by the very ones who crucified him, as well as by the crowd, as having divine attributes that lifted him beyond the level of a criminal, and even beyond the level of religious or fanatical cult leader. These witnesses, in other words, made disinterested claims on Jesus' behalf which were in contradiction to what the Sanhedrin said about him before and after his death and resurrection.

Sometimes in our zeal for good theology and solid biblical teaching, we ignore or reject the Baalams, persons who give testimonials to the mystery of spiritual realities despite being obviously unqualified to do so. Instead, when these are a part of God's redeeming work in the life of an individual or group, we would do well to listen respectfully and give credence whether or not they appear to be of our number. There are lots of "unqualified" witnesses to be found in various Bible narratives.

These witnesses at the cross are many, although one is especially cited. According to the Old Testament judicial standards, two or three witnesses were needed to fix an important matter. But more generally, God usually does things for individuals in the context of their relationships. We are made for fellowship with God and with one another. Our lives and testimonies are meant to be in the plural. There is a power in group experience and in sharing personal accounts

7.

of God's working. Few things can match our combined accounts for credibility. In the words of an old country hymn, "It is no secret what God can do/ What he's done for me he can do for you." The testimony of unbelievers who have caught a first glimpse of the kingdom can be particularly precious.

Chapter Two: Despite The Cost

-- The women at the cross and John

Matthew 27:55-56
55 And many women were there beholding afar off, which followed Jesus from Galilee, ministering unto him:
56 Among whom was Mary Magdalene, and Mary the mother of James and Joses, and the mother of Zebedee's children.

Mark 15:40-41
40 There were also women looking on afar off: among whom was Mary Magdalene, and Mary the mother of James the less and of Joses, and Salome,
41 (Who also, when he was in Galilee, followed him, and ministered unto him;) and many other women which came up with him unto Jerusalem.

Luke 23:27-28, 48
27 And there followed him a great company of people, and of women, which also bewailed and lamented him.
28 But Jesus turning to them said, Daughters of Jerusalem, weep not for me, but weep for yourselves, and for your children.
. . .
48 And all his acquaintance, and the women that followed him from Galilee, stood afar off, beholding these things.

John 19:25-27
25 Now there stood by the cross of Jesus his mother, and his mother's sister, Mary the wife of Cleophas, and Mary Magdalene.
26 When Jesus therefore saw his mother, and the disciple standing by, whom he loved, he saith unto his mother, Woman, behold thy son!
27 Then he saith to the disciple, Behold thy mother! And from that hour that disciple took her unto his own home.

The Bible does not teach the "equality of the sexes" in all matters, despite what some would have us believe. The crucifixion accounts give solid evidence for the superiority of women in perseverance and faithfulness. So far as we can tell, the only one of the twelve disciples of Christ to be present at the crucifixion was John. But we find record of at least four of the women who followed him,: Mary, Jesus' mother; Mary Magdalene; Mary, the wife of Cleophas; and Salome.

First it seems likely these women -- and a large company of others with them -- followed Jesus on the Via Dolorosa, as he went to his execution. They were weeping and mourning, apparently in great sorrow over the prospect. He turns to them, however, and says, in effect, 'You're weeping for the wrong person. You ought to be weeping for yourselves, for Jerusalem, and for Israel'. It is a two-sided statement: on the purely human side, it means simply that his death is more of a tragedy as it reflects on the spiritual state of others than an ultimate tragedy for him. But equally as pointedly, it seems to be a prophecy of the destruction to come on his beloved Jerusalem, of which his crucifixion was in a sense a harbinger.

The crowd at Golgotha itself must have ebbed and flowed. We have already read (Luke 23:48) that the people "came together at that sight". We know there had been a crowd of some sort gathered before Pilate, a crowd which called for Barabbas' release and Jesus' crucifixion, but this is not the same crowd. (In fact some commentators have said only a small crowd could have fit in the narrow courtyard occupied by those calling "crucify".) This crowd is larger and more sympathetic, but probably few believe Jesus to be the Messiah. They have come together around the commotion – as a crowd will. At least in part, they also see Jesus' crucifixion as one more injustice amidst the general injustice of Roman rule. For most of them, resentment against the ruling powers fuels what sympathy they may have, as much as love or admiration.

The women and John stand, for a while, far away from the cross itself. "All his acquaintance" also stand afar off. (Are these the other disciples, already returning, ashamed of their denials and their flights? If so, they kept far enough away that no record of their names was recorded.) Perhaps the soldiers kept them back, as "peace-keepers" instinctively seem to do any time a crowd gathers around some object or event. Perhaps the initial crowd was so large that the women could not get nearer. Certainly some of them continued to be afraid to be identified with Jesus, the criminal. This fear cannot have dominated all, however, for there is ample evidence that many of his followers boldly began to identify as his again soon after his death.

They draw nearer, in any case, for despite his gradual asphyxiation as he is hanging on the cross, Jesus is able to address them -- specifically his mother and John. At the near climax of his suffering for our sins, he has time of mind and room of heart to care for the details of his earthly responsibilities -- formalizing an adoptive relationship between two of the people he most loved in this world. To them this must have been intensely poignant -- that as his life ebbs away and his ministry comes to an ultimate failure (for they did not yet understand its success), he still ministers selflessly. But a further, as yet invisible-to-them, facet of his compassion lies in assigning John to Mary. John is assigned to be his replacement in protection and comfort, but also his replacement as an earthly son, since Jesus is to rise and ascend back to heaven.

The other women are faithful, too. Some of the bonds which keep them close to a failed visionary (for this is all Jesus must seem to most of them at this point) are bonds of relationship: family, ministry, and combinations of these. They are together. It is often said that "misery loves company," but as the Apostle Paul tells us,

> . . . whether one member suffer, all the members suffer with it; or one member be honoured, all the members

rejoice with it.   Now ye are the body of Christ, and members particularly.   (I Corinthians 12:26-7)

The body of Christ is torn and bleeding, dying on the cross – but at the same time the Body of Christ is being strengthened and bound together – as it still is, through suffering (and soon through rejoicing).   The sorrow of the faithful over what appears to be final events of their fellowship is a further bond in what is to be an eternal fellowship.

While it may be true that women have always been faithful and courageous in identifying with those they love, and while it may be true that women are often treated with a higher degree of tolerance by high-handed rulers (perhaps because such feel less threatened by women than by men) it is nevertheless true these women are behaving in a manner not explicable in ordinary terms.   That many another woman has behaved similarly in similar circumstances before and since does not dispel the mystery.

In that much beloved classic of our generation, *The Lord of the Rings*, a scene of similar high pathos comes just after the climax in which the ring is cast into the Cracks of Doom and destroyed.   Frodo and Sam, exhausted in bodies, minds and spirits, make their way back down the slopes of Mount Doom. There they expect to perish momentarily in the cataclysmic fall of mountain and magma around them.   There is comfort for them even at this moment, however, in their companionship. Frodo says to Sam, "I am glad you are here with me. Here at the end of all things, Sam."

Of course Frodo was proved wrong – but we do not well to rush on in life when things appear to be ending. When those we love struggle with the perception that we are "here at the end of all things," we may make the mistake of scrambling about so furiously trying to prove them wrong, that we fail to meet their need for real companions and friends in that hour.

In some measure these women must have been conscious of the potential cost of identifying with Jesus at his ignoble death, yet they persevered and stood together as witnesses who loved Jesus -- the faithful complementing those other witnesses around the cross.

It is an old way of speaking, but a sure one – the place we need to be when we feel we are at "the end of all things" is near the cross. And if in the darkness of our circumstances or our souls Jesus seems to us inaccessible, we should gather together in the last place where he spoke to us.

When It Was Yet Dark

Chapter Three: From Fearful To Fools

-- Joseph of Arimathea and Nicodemus,
and the women at the tomb

Matthew 27:57-60
57 When the even was come, there came a rich man of Arimathaea, named Joseph, who also himself was Jesus' disciple:
58 He went to Pilate, and begged the body of Jesus. Then Pilate commanded the body to be delivered.
59 And when Joseph had taken the body, he wrapped it in a clean linen cloth,
60 And laid it in his own new tomb, which he had hewn out in the rock: and he rolled a great stone to the door of the sepulchre, and departed.

Mark 15:42-47
42 And now when the even was come, because it was the preparation, that is, the day before the sabbath,
43 Joseph of Arimathaea, an honourable counselor, which also waited for the kingdom of God, came, and went in boldly unto Pilate, and craved the body of Jesus.
44 And Pilate marveled if he were already dead: and calling unto him the centurion, he asked him whether he had been any while dead.
45 And when he knew it of the centurion, he gave the body to Joseph.
46 And he bought fine linen, and took him down, and wrapped him in the linen, and laid him in a sepulchre which was hewn out of a rock, and rolled a stone unto the door of the sepulchre.

Luke 23:50-54
50 And behold, there was a man named Joseph, a counselor, and he was a good man, and a just:
51 (The same had not consented to the counsel and deed of them;) he was of Arimathaea, a city of the Jews: who also himself waited for the kingdom of God.
52 This man went to Pilate, and begged the body of Jesus.
53 And he took it down, and wrapped it in linen, and laid it in a sepulchre that was hewn in stone, wherein never man before was laid.
54 And that day was the preparation, and the sabbath drew on.

John 19:38-42

38 And after this Joseph of Arimathaea, being a disciple of Jesus, but secretly for fear of the Jews, besought Pilate that he might take away the body of Jesus: and Pilate gave him leave. He came therefore, and took the body of Jesus.

39 And there came also Nicodemus, which at first came to Jesus by night, and brought a mixture of myrrh and aloes, about an hundred pound weight.

40 Then took they the body of Jesus, and wound it in linen clothes with the spices, as the manner of the Jews is to bury.

41 Now in the place where he was crucified there was a garden; and in the garden a new sepulchre, wherein was never man yet laid.

42 There laid they Jesus therefore because of the Jews' preparation day; for the sepulchre was nigh at hand.

Here we see two more "disciples" publicly identifying with the Lord at the worst possible moment -- that is after his death and apparent defeat -- and after his execution, at the height of the moment when he and his associates are publicly recognized as criminals, and repudiated by the Jewish leaders. Nor do these two, Joseph and Nicodemus, have a record for special courage and faithfulness.

Joseph of Arimathaea is not spoken of by name in any passage other than the four above. We read that he was a rich man, an honorable counselor, a disciple of Jesus, one waiting for the kingdom of God to come, and a good and just man. We also find that as a member of the Sanhedrin he did not consent to that council's decisions -- to have Jesus arrested and to pursue his execution, apparently. However, we have not only the silence of scripture, (not in itself reliable evidence) to tell us Joseph was previously a fearful believer, but also the statement in John's gospel that he was a believer who kept his faith secret out of fear of the Jews. In our day we would say he had caved in to social or peer pressure -- if only to the extent of being afraid to be known as a follower of this unpopular teacher by the other leaders in Jerusalem. His "darkness" was the shadow of human opinion, the dread of the loneliness and insecurity which results when one openly breaks with his contemporaries.

Nicodemus is known to us more fully in that we have two earlier accounts of him (John 3:1-9ff and John 7:50). He, too, was a Pharisee and a religious leader. It was he who came to Jesus with some compliments and a few important questions -- questions to which Jesus replied in some of the most quoted of scriptures. But Nicodemus came to Jesus by night. All three passages which mention him tell us this -- in fact, this has become his identifying description in both John chapters 7 and 19. He, too, was afraid of being openly identified with Jesus. Caution has been the essence of his character -- he came by night, "in the dark" – while it was yet dark – although he had lots of well-thought out questions. He responded to each of Jesus' answers with further searching questions (including reasonable objections), and we may even detect between the lines the frustration of a cautious person being told bold and difficult things. Finally, when Jesus is about to be condemned by the Council, he objects -- on the basis of the law, but also, perhaps, because by nature he feels it is wrong to rush into anything – and especially this thing.

It is in response to Nicodemus' questions that Jesus tells us no man enters the kingdom of God without being born again. It is in response to Nicodemus that Jesus tells us that God so loved the world that he gave his only begotten son that whosoever believeth on him should not perish but have everlasting life. But in those passages, this same Nicodemus gives no evidence of being "born again" or believing in Jesus as the only begotten son. He testifies Jesus is "a teacher come from God," and that "God is with" Jesus – on the basis of the miracles Jesus has performed. But Jesus receives these compliments as though 'damned with faint praise'. He is abrupt and challenging in his responses. Later Nicodemus' objection in the Council is courageous, but it may be, as it were, as much the courage of caution as the courage of faith.

Few things are more frustrating to us than half-hearted friends. At how many points do we in the church deserve to hear what the Lord tells the Laodicean church in Revelations chapter three, "I would that you were cold or hot!" Or how many times do the faithful in the church wish their leaders would quit shilly-shallying and stand up for Christ like men. But Jesus will not quench the smouldering wicks nor break the bruised reeds. He rejects neither Judas nor Peter at several points where you and I surely would have.

In his disturbing and powerful novel, *Silence*, Shusako Endo portrays a pusillanimous and traitorous "believer" who sells out the priests and the church in Japan not just once but a number of times. When the traitor seeks forgiveness and reconciliation yet once more, the one whom he has betrayed goes through a great struggle. This becomes one of the key places where Christ's man has to affirm or deny the gospel. So with us – how quickly would Joseph of Arimathaea or Nicodemus be admitted into our fellowship? Would we welcome the participation of these two compromisers in the rites honoring our Lord? (One of the greatest issues that was to trouble the church of the first centuries was how to treat the "lapsed," those who denied Christ during pagan persecutions, and then sought to be readmitted to Christian fellowship.)

But now we see these two careful, cautious, and essentially cowardly men become bold – yea, from the world's standpoint, they begin acting like fools! Matthew and Luke say that Joseph begged the body; Mark tells us he went in boldly before Pilate to do so. These two minority members of a religious and political body powerful enough to induce the governor to put an innocent man to death, decide at the moment a cause has collapsed to go before that governor in broad daylight and identify with that cause, asking for the body of its leader in order that they might honor it with the rites of burial.

Nicodemus had said to the council, "Doth our law judge any man, before it hear him, and know what he doeth?" (John 7:51) Deep in his heart, that instinctive tendency to cut and run had been restrained to his own counsel. He and Joseph, without a rational hope in the world, kept on faithful, indeed grew more faithful, waiting for what they did not know -- the full revelation of what Jesus had said and done -- what he would do. Like Abraham their father, they went into a land they did not know. They walked blindly by faith into insecurity, one step at time.

Their love for Jesus is expressed in the humblest and one might almost say the lowest and least significant of services -- ministry to his dead body. Joseph offers the best thing he can for a dead man -- an unused, newly-hewn tomb set in a garden. Nicodemus brings the ingredients for embalming and the two of them wrap the body of Jesus in fine linen and lay it in the grave.

The devotion of these acts has become foreign to us whose dead are always prepared for burial by professionals. Larry Woiwode's novel *Born Brothers* contains a wonderful passage in which a son prepares his father's body for burial. The passage succeeds in depicting a similar timelessness poised in the here-and-now, a tender devotion to what is and what has been, without regard for what may be tomorrow. Reading it gives one a deeper sense of the love of Joseph and Nicodemus. But while Woiwode's character performs his rite alone, Joseph and Nicodemus perform this ministry together. Like the women, their companionship is part of their faithfulness.

What led these pusillanimous men to this bold stand? What led these men who had been so careful to remain secret to openly identify with Jesus? What kept them going when any sensible person would have retreated completely and retrenched into the security of agreement with peers and repudiation of the alien?

Whatever it was it is also at work in our lives and hearts at those times and places when we can think of no reason whatever to keep on acting faithfully, when our past compromises, our frustrations, and our fear of men cajole us to fade quietly into the woodwork.

When It Was Yet Dark

Chapter Four: The Wrong Way Wiser

– Judas

Matthew 27:3-10
3 Then Judas, which had betrayed him, when he saw that he was condemned, repented himself, and brought again the thirty pieces of silver to the chief priests and elders,
4 Saying, I have sinned in that I have betrayed the innocent blood. And they said, What is that to us? See thou to that.
5 And he cast down the pieces of silver in the temple, and departed, and went and hanged himself.
6 And the chief priests took the silver pieces, and said, It is not lawful for to put them into the treasury, because it is the price of blood.
7 And they took counsel, and bought with them the potter's field, to bury strangers in.
8 Wherefore that field was called, The field of blood, unto this day.
9 Then was it fulfilled that which was spoken by Jeremy the prophet, saying, And they took the thirty pieces of silver, the price of him that was valued, whom they of the children of Israel did value;
10 and gave them for the potter's field, as the Lord appointed me.

Judas is a difficult character for us to deal with. He is a good litmus test of our theology -- are we going to take the easy way out, the way of just labeling him a "bad apple"? (This division of people into good and bad groups has risen to epidemic proportions in our times, but it is not tenable for the Christian.) Or will we be facile in distant compassion? It were better that we seek to be biblical about him. Dorothy Sayers in her series of plays, *The Man Born To Be King*, depicts Judas as a political activist, one whose chief conscious motive is stirring Jesus to use his full power to overthrow the Roman oppressors. His act of betrayal, as Sayers portrays it, is partly intended to incite or precipitate an open war. In her treatment it is clearly Judas' expectation that Jesus will finally use his divine power to establish himself as king, provoked at last by his arrest. After all, Jesus has talked about this "Kingdom of God" over and over again. Subsequent dramatic treatments of the gospel narrative have utilized this same set of motives for Judas. He becomes a Barabbas-like character, a revolutionary or political radical. The chiefest biblical support for such a perspective is found in what Matthew tells us, that Judas "repented" when Jesus was condemned and delivered up to Pilate for execution.

There is value in exploring perspectives which bring Judas' actions home to us, so that we see our own sin in him, but it is important we not lose track of what the scriptures themselves say. Judas, whatever his political affinities, was a very selfish man. Jesus speaks of him in the abstract as "a devil". We read that he was the treasurer among Jesus' disciples, and a thief. In common with the other disciples he did not like the "waste" of the alabaster jar full of precious ointment which Mary broke and poured out to anoint Jesus, but unlike them, his expressed concern that the money be used for the poor is apparently hypocritical, and mere cover for avarice.

He betrays Jesus for thirty pieces of silver -- and the simplest explanation of an immediate motive is avarice again. But two passages tell us Judas was also under an intense influence of the devil -- much as King Saul was in his murderous rages against David. His behavior cannot all be due to "higher" or ideological motives of bringing about revolution against oppressive tyrants. (I don't think Sayers indicates it's only that.) The best literary treatments of Judas rightly make him a complex character, while avoiding the modern error of making complexity equivalent to virtue. In the end betrayal is a simple thing – it is simply evil. Faithfulness is a simple thing – it is simply good. In that hallowed period of his Passion, Jesus saw a great deal more of the one than the other.

If we wish to emphasize the things about Judas which make him "human" to us, we must also emphasize his unfaithfulness to his Savior, and more important yet, we ought to emphasize the wrong choice he made after it became clear to him that what he had done was wrong. Up to that point he was another sinner, one among the complete number of unfaithful disciples, though he may have been the most actively traitorous.

Judas' greatest sin was not betraying Jesus. It was committing suicide. It sounds strange to say it is worse to kill yourself than to help kill the Son of God, but such is the fact. Judas' most terrible deed was his refusal to repent in godly sorrow in reaffirmation of his Lord. Instead he destroyed himself in a high-handed, unrepentant, self-willed act contrary to the express will of God.

Whatever his scheme may have been when he betrayed Jesus, it was being wise the wrong way. Likewise his response as he saw the results of that betrayal. His "repentance" was a worldly and self-willed repentance, not a repentance unto life, such as the Apostle Paul describes to the Corinthian church:

> Now I rejoice, not that ye were made sorry, but that ye sorrowed to repentance: for ye were made sorry after a godly manner, that ye might receive damage by us in nothing. For godly sorrow worketh repentance to salvation not to be repented of: but the sorrow of the world worketh death. (II Corinthians 7:9-10)

Judas' sorrow was a sorrow of the world. It was essentially more of the same – his own best idea of what would work, what would be appropriate, what would fix the mess he had made. Murder is a great evil. Self-murder is murder. Like abortion and euthanasia, it is taking the law in our own hands and making ourselves like God. I have a good friend who struggled with suicidal thoughts at many of the more difficult points of her life. She found it a great blessing to make a "non-suicide pact," a written commitment not to commit self-murder and to thus share her struggles with others who entered into that "contract" with her. Her sorrows were real. Like Peter she knew a deep sense of having done wrong. Both she and Peter knew as much about sorrow as Judas. But they shared their grief and guilt with others and with the Lord. As in the traditions of some pagan cultures, Judas' self-murder was an effort to "save face". He would not humble himself before God and thought to escape God in death. Even Shakespeare's Hamlet, despite great confusion, reasoned better than that.

Judas is one of the loneliest men in the Bible. Had he shared his heart, his doubts, his fears, his desires, his lusts, his sorrow, and his confusion with one other, his story would have been different.

Lord Jesus, we too are betrayers -- along with Judas, and Peter, and all the others. Give us grace to turn to you in godly sorrow and to share our lives and hearts with others that they may help us to keep our sorrow godly.

May God also deliver us from pettifogging about the smaller tokens of sin. Keep us from penitential efforts to turn bad into good, as though the proper incantations made over blood money could turn it into an offering to a righteous God. Deliver us from Pharisaical complicity, participation, or support at any level of those who kill claiming to love – whether it be to kill old men and babies in the name of love, or to kill the Son of God in the name of love. Where we have sinned, grant us a godly repentance.

Chapter Five: Angels and Dead Men

-- Angelic agents, angelic messengers, and the risen dead

Matthew 27:51-53

51 And behold, the vail of the temple was rent in twain from the top to the bottom; and the earth did quake, and the rocks rent;

52 And the graves were opened; and many bodies of the saints which slept arose,

53 And came out of the graves after his resurrection, and went into the holy city, and appeared unto many.

Matthew 28: 1-7

1 In the end of the sabbath, as it began to dawn toward the first day of the week, came Mary Magdalene and the other Mary to see the sepulchre.

2 And behold, there was a great earthquake: for the angel of the Lord descended from heaven, and came and rolled back the stone from the door, and sat upon it.

3 His countenance was like lightning, and his raiment white as snow:

4 And for fear of him the keepers did shake, and became as dead men.

5 And the angel answered and said unto the women, Fear not ye: for I know that ye seek Jesus, which was crucified.

6 He is not here: for he is risen, as he said. Come, see the place where the Lord lay.

7 Go quickly, and tell his disciples that he is risen from the dead; and behold, he goeth before you into Galilee; there shall ye see him: lo, I have told you.

Mark 16:4-8

[Mary Magdalene, Mary the mother of James, and Salome came to the tomb asking themselves who would roll away the stone for them]

4 And when they looked, they saw that the stone was rolled away: for it was very great.

5 And entering into the sepulchre, they saw a young man sitting on the right side, clothed in a long white garment; and they were affrighted.

6 And he saith unto them, Be not affrighted: Ye seek Jesus of Nazareth, which was crucified: he is risen; he is not here: behold the place where they laid him.

7 But go your way, tell his disciples and Peter that he goeth before you into Galilee: there shall ye see him, as he said unto you.

8 And they went out quickly, and fled from the sepulchre; for they trembled and were amazed: neither said they any thing to any man; for they were afraid.

Luke 24:2-9
[The women came to the tomb]
2 And they found the stone rolled away from the sepulchre.
3 And they entered in, and found not the body of the Lord Jesus.
4 And it came to pass, as they were much perplexed thereabout, behold, two men stood by them in shining garments:
5 And as they were afraid, and bowed down their faces to the earth, they said unto them, Why seek ye the living among the dead?
6 He is not here, but is risen: remember how he spake unto you when he was yet in Galilee,
7 Saying, the Son of man must be delivered unto the hands of sinful men, and be crucified, and the third day rise again.
8 And they remembered his words.
9 And returned from the sepulchre, and told all these things unto the eleven, and to all the rest.

Luke 24: 22-23 (the two men on the road to Emmaus retail the events)
22 Yea, and certain women also of our company made us astonished, which were early at the sepulchre;
23 And when they found not his body, they came, saying, that they had also seen a vision of angels, which said that he was alive.

Angels and dead men are among the dramatic witnesses to God's grace when it is manifested. Indeed, if we look back through the witnesses of God's power and grace we find angels and dead men testifying from near the beginning. An angel with a burning sword stands at the entrance of Eden after the fall, and dead Abel's blood testifies from the ground. An angel of the Lord comes to God's people at other key moments: one came to Abraham before the destruction of Sodom and Gomorrah, and to Joshua before the destruction of Jericho. Dead men testified at several weird moments in Old Testament history – the ghost of Samuel tells Saul the Lord has departed from him and that he and his sons will be killed the next day (I Samuel 28), and a dead man thrown into the tomb of Elisha is brought back to life when he touches the old prophet's bones.

But even more important are the angels and dead men surrounding Jesus' ministry. It was an angel that addressed Mary with the gentle but incredible news that she was to bear the baby Immanuel. God spoke similarly to Joseph. We love the story of the angels that came to the shepherds when he was born. Perhaps these at the tomb are the same ones!

We also know of the dead innocent children of Bethlehem, in a strange way substitutes, but also prophets of Jesus' death.

From the gospels, we know about three dead people who have been raised by Jesus : first the son of the widow of Nain, whom he raises as the body is being borne away on a stretcher; then Jairus' daughter (Jairus was the ruler of a synagogue in a town of Galilee) whom he raises after being laughed at for saying she was only asleep; and finally Lazarus his friend and the brother of Mary and Martha. Jesus also wept over Lazarus' grave before calling out his name – by which word and power Lazarus came forth alive from the dead. (Lazarus was raised after being <u>four</u> days dead, and according to the accounts, the Lord deliberately dawdled in coming there. Perhaps Jesus wanted to make sure we recognized the distinctions between Lazarus' resurrection and Jesus own. For surely Lazarus died again later (or rather "fell asleep") whereas Jesus rose after <u>three</u> (the number of perfection) days, beyond which he lives eternally, death having no more dominion.

The Matthew account puts the tearing of the Temple veil and the tearing of the very rocks of earth in the same verses. Both are works of heaven (the veil is torn from the top to the bottom, not bottom to top, as it would have been had men done it). Both open up ways formerly closed. The veil of the Temple was the barrier before the Holy of Holies, that sacrosanct place in the temple where no one could go but the high priest and only once a year after intensive purification. The earth and rocks seem to be particularly those surrounding graves – barriers put there by the living to separate them from the dead, but also, in another figurative sense, symbolic of the barrier between life and death, which no one had climbed over before, except apparently Enoch and Elijah.

Teachers have thought a great deal about the symbolism of the torn veil. It shows us that the separation between man and God, chiefly through man's sin and God's unapproachable holiness, has been removed through Jesus' death. His sacrifice for sin has made a way for us "through the vail, that is to say, his flesh" into the Holy of Holies (Hebrews 10:20) once and for all.

In addition to the angels, these dead testify as well. They do not remain outside the city where all the graves are – but they go into the city. Since I am more of a poet than a theologian, I will make the tentative suggestion that perhaps they are headed for the temple, perhaps going through the torn veil into that sacramental place of God's presence, witnessing by their mysterious and frightening pilgrimage to the full efficacy of Jesus work on the cross. Wherever they were headed or whatever they were up to, many people saw them. A breach had been made in the wall between the dead and the living. The cataclysms of heaven, earth, and Sheol must have kept the citizens of Jerusalem pretty nervous during those three days.

We have already read of the meteorological phenomena and earthquakes as Jesus died. But now the night (or nights) of the living dead followed Jesus resurrection. There was another (at least one more) earthquake, however -- apparently at the same time as the angel rolled the stone from the grave. These combined phenomena are so frightening as to paralyze the guards at the tomb into complete immobility, what I think we might call a catatonic state.

The angels frighten everyone who sees them, with the exception, apparently, of Mary Magdalene who is already so deeply preoccupied in grief and worry (see the next section) that (according to John's gospel) she doesn't seem to notice they are angels. They have faces bright (or flashing?) like lightning, but they tell the witnesses not to fear. So we, in those yet-dark places where God breaks in, have a natural tendency to shrink away in fear – to avoid the very light we have been asking for – manifestations of his love and power.

When It Was Yet Dark

Chapter Six: When It Was Yet Dark

– Mary Magdalene and the other women;
then Peter and John at the tomb

Mark 16:1-11

1 And when the sabbath was past, Mary Magdalene, and Mary the mother of James, and Salome had bought sweet spices, that they might come and anoint him.

2 And very early in the morning the first day of the week, they came unto the sepulchre at the rising of the sun.

3 And they said among themselves, Who shall roll us away the stone from the door of the sepulchre?

4 And when they looked, they saw that the stone was rolled away: for it was very great.

5 And entering into the sepulchre, they saw a young man sitting on the right side, clothed in a long white garment; and they were affrighted.

6 And he saith unto them, Be not affrighted: Ye seek Jesus of Nazareth, which was crucified: he is risen; he is not here: behold the place where they laid him.

7 But go your way, tell his disciples and Peter that he goeth before you into Galilee: there shall ye see him, as he said unto you.

8 And they went out quickly, and fled from the sepulchre; for they trembled and were amazed: neither said they any thing to any man; for they were afraid.

9 Now when Jesus was risen early the first day of the week, he appeared first to Mary Magdalene, out of whom he had cast seven devils.

10 And she went and told them that had been with him, as they mourned and wept.

11 And they, when they heard that he was alive, and had been seen of her believed not.

Matthew 28:1-10

1 In the end of the sabbath, as it began to dawn toward the first day of the week, came Mary Magdalene and the other Mary to see the sepulchre.

2 And, behold, there was a great earthquake: for the angel of the Lord descended from heaven, and came and rolled back the stone from the door, and sat upon it

3 His countenance was like lightning, and his raiment white as snow:

4 And for fear of him the keepers did shake, and became like dead men.

5 And the angel answered and said unto the women, Fear not ye: for I know that ye seek Jesus, which was crucified.

6 He is not here: for he is risen, as he said. Come, see the place where the Lord lay.

7 And go quickly, and tell his disciples that he is risen from the dead; and, behold, he goeth before you into Galilee; there shall ye see him: lo, I have told you.

8 And they departed quickly from the sepulchre with fear and great joy; and did run to bring his disciples word.

(Luke 24:1-12; 22-24)

John 20:1-18

1 The first day of the week cometh Mary Magdalene early, when it was yet dark, unto the sepulcher, and seeth the stone taketh away from the sepulcher.

2 Then she runneth, and cometh to Simon Peter, and to the other disciple, whom Jesus loved, and saith unto them, They have taken away the Lord out of the sepulcher, and we know not where they have laid him.

3 Peter therefore went forth, and that other disciple, and came to the sepulcher.

4 So they ran both together: and the other disciple did outrun Peter, and came first to the sepulcher.

5 And he stooping down, and looking in, saw the linen clothes lying; yet went he not in.

6 Then cometh Simon Peter following him, and went into the sepulcher, and seeth the linen clothes lie,

7 And the napkin, that was about his head, not lying with the linen clothes, but wrapped together in a place by itself.

8 Then went in also that other disciple, which came first to the sepulcher, and he saw, and believed.

9 For as yet they knew not the scripture, that he must rise again from the dead.

10 Then the disciples went away again unto their home.

11 But Mary stood without at the sepulcher weeping: and as she wept, she stopped down, and looked into the sepulcher,

12 And seeth two angels in white sitting, the one at the head. And the other at the feet. Where the body of Jesus had lain.

13 And they say unto her, Woman, why weepest thou? She saith unto them, Because they have taken away my Lord, and I know not where they have laid him.

14 And when she had thus said, she turned herself back, and saw Jesus standing, and knew not that it was Jesus.

15 Jesus saith unto her, Woman, why weepest thou? Whom seekest thou? She, supposing him to be the gardener, saith unto him, Sir, if thou have borne him hence, tell me where thou hast laid him, and I will take him away.
16 Jesus saith unto her, Mary. She turned herself, and saith unto him, Rabboni; which is to say, Master.
17 Jesus saith unto her, Touch me not; for I am not yet ascended to my Father: but go to my brethren, and say unto them, I ascend unto my Father, and your Father; and to my God, and your God.
18 Mary Magdalene came and told the disciples that she had seen the Lord, and that he had spoken these things unto her.

The title for this book is taken from the time and conditions under which Mary Magdalene came to the tomb. But I have projected the term and have been using it in three ways:

- Mary's coming to the tomb – history, fact, time and place;
- Mary's heart and faith -- that is still "in the dark" and representative of all the disciples at the time;
- The "dark times" of our trials and confusion parallel to these. Mary's darkened faith is thus representative for all the rest of us at such times.

Mary Magdalene is highly honored, much as Mary the mother was, in being the chosen bearer of unbelievable news and hope. She is the first firsthand witness of the resurrected Jesus. She is the very first person to whom he speaks thereafter. She is not a virgin, but rather a former prostitute. She is not "holy" by virtue of a lifelong self-restraint and ancient record of faithful obedience, but in some new way – as redeemed and transformed. This ought to excite us who know a little of our own fallen natures. We ought to know a similar joy to that we feel in reading Jesus' words to the thief on the cross – "This day will you be with me in paradise," though the thief had none of the requirements of decent religion, not even baptism, nor any record of good deeds -- only a childlike faith.

Mary Magdalene is honored and blessed by God, and we must bear this in mind as we study this passage. She is also very much a picture of how we respond to life "when it is yet dark," and in order to know ourselves sinners, we ought to focus on those things, too.

In this chapter, then, I'm going to pick on Mary a little – not because she is different from us, but because she is the same. Her ways of coping are our ways. Her mechanisms and defenses for dealing with life gone out-of-control are very much ours.

1/ We forget what the Lord has done in the past. Mary Magdalene comes to the tomb to anoint Jesus body for burial. Perhaps she has done this once before, by his own testimony. Although she is not named in the passage, it is conjectured by many that she is the woman, "which was a sinner" in Luke 7:36-50, who anoints his feet with her tears and precious ointment, and about whom Jesus confronts Simon the Pharisee with the parable of the two debtors.

But now the Mary "who was forgiven much" sees the stone rolled away, and the body missing, and not much more. Her eyes work twenty-twenty, but are not connecting with her memory. She's seen empty tombs before. But her knowledge of things unseen is in abeyance. In her dejection, she is relying on earthly experience of the "normal" world rather than the real , but spiritual, record of God's grace which she has known. This has a strong parallel in John the Baptist's doubting while in Herod's prison – on which occasion, some time after his great testimony to Jesus as Messiah, he sends messengers to inquire if Jesus really is the one. Yesterday's great faith is no guarantee against today's unbelief. We cannot rest on our own past record – but we can find comfort in the Lord's record of grace toward us. (And if we find ourselves doubting, who better to inquire of?)

Mary Magdalene (and the other women in the other gospels) came to the grave without the tiniest expectation of finding anything but a cold body behind a cold stone door.

This means she (and they – and the men, too, of course) had forgotten not only what the Lord had said quite recently, but what he had done. The category "risen from the dead," was not operating for them, even though Jesus had raised three people from the dead during his ministry (and probably many more). She had even heard Jesus taunted in those terms as he hung on the cross – yet she had not the slightest hope or expectation that he himself might rise from the dead. This shows through in the rest of her "coping" mechanisms.

Furthermore, Mary has personally experienced amazing grace at Jesus' hands. We read that it was she out of whom he cast seven devils. (Mark 10:9, Luke 8:2) She has known his spiritual power over death and the devil – but seems to have lost track of it now.

2/ **We cling to the visible remnants of what we once hoped for** rather than renewing our hope by faith. Mary and the other women (along with Joseph of Arimathaea, Nicodemus, Peter and John et al) are devoted to the body of Jesus. I have no intention of entering into controversy with my Catholic brethren over "devotion to the body of Christ" as they use that term today. But they will agree with me that if Christ were not raised from the dead, devotion to his body would be no more meaningful than devotion to the body of Confucius, Buddha, or Mohammed. In other words, I am arguing that the devotion of the followers of Christ in these passages, in contrast to what comes later, is not driven principally by intentional faith, but that on the contrary, they are only conscious of a kind of nostalgia. She is not there believing in what is, but mourning what was by ministering to "the remains".

One must be tremendously careful about forbidding mourning. John Donne's great love poem "A Valediction: Forbidding Mourning" is not really that, but rather an affirmation of relationship that bridges parting. Dylan Thomas' great mourning poem "Do Not Go Gentle Into That Good Night," calls his dying father to "rage, rage against the dying of the light". Yet we know it is the poet who rages against death in general and his father's death in particular. Further, we know that raging in this way is only a re-directed (and futile) form of mourning. To mourn is legitimate. We read in Romans 8 that the whole creation groans, that we ourselves legitimately groan, and that the Holy Spirit intercedes for us with groans too deep for words. All this groaning is over two things – the way things are and the fact that they are not yet what they ought to be. When a friend loses a loved one, we ought to mourn with him – sometimes too deeply for words, which will be made evident in our few words.

But we need to examine our own mourning carefully – are we mourning what is and what was without reference to what will be? Are we bustling about in "devotion" to what or whom we lost -- without faith? Is our bustling in fact a tactic or even a strategy to avoid dealing with anger, fear, and unbelief? Is there a part of us that would rather anoint a dead body than meet a resurrected one? If so, we are not spending our time as we ought. No spices, no secret formula, no fine linen fabric will preserve what is truly dead. Nor can they hold back what is truly living.

3/ We jump to wrong conclusions. Mary finds the stone rolled away. (Indeed, in the Matthew account we are told the women saw the angel roll back the stone and sit on it!) Yet Mary, perhaps slightly demented by the spectacular phenomena (although to a lesser degree than the guards!) upon discovering Jesus' body gone, concludes that it has been stolen!

How often when things are wrong in our lives we leap to conclusions wildly at odds with faith! 'God is being cruel to me!' 'God has robbed me!' 'If God loved me, this would never have happened!' Or more subtly -- 'My enemies have been allowed to triumph over me.' (Consider how the psalmist struggles with such feelings!)

So set are we on remaining in control of our existence, that no matter how mightily we are shaken, we fight to the last for the right to jump to wrong conclusions, and to cling to them. Mary takes this "body-snatcher" theory to its ultimate ridiculous climax. So often we do the same with theories born purely out of our coping instincts.

It is particularly notable that Mary explains the difficulties that confront her with a conspiracy theory. "They" have taken Jesus body. "They" have hidden it. The chief errors in her conclusion continue among us. First, that human agencies are more powerful than God. Second, that human agencies are capable of the extreme measures which our fearful imaginations attribute to them. Third, that "figuring out" the details of these imagined conspiracies is very important and will be a key step in somehow overcoming them.

Every Christian and all Christian groups are susceptible to the foolishness of conspiracy-worship. And worship it is! What else should we call it when something becomes central to our thought to the point that the Lord is no longer central. Some Catholics are convinced the Masons are behind many evils. Many Protestants suggest it's the Catholics, or the Jews, or the Illuminati, or the rich bankers, or whomever. It's so much easier to focus on a "seen" enemy, or at least one with a label and description, than to resist the devil, flee temptation, repent of sin, and be in the world but not of it. For these are our enemies: world, flesh (with sin in the flesh), and the devil.

Between the time this writing was first drafted and the time it was finished Y2K came and went. The great catastrophes predicted proved to be a tempest in a teapot. Oh, yes, there are enemies of God deliberately and actively pursuing policies in opposition to his revealed will, his law and his people, but they aren't worth as much attention as we give them. The Lord has told us a kingdom divided against itself cannot stand – and Satan's kingdom is by its very essence such a kingdom.

God does not see conspiracies where we naturally do – and tells us we are not to conform ourselves to the conspiracies theories of others. (See also Isaiah 8:12-13)

4/ We get busy.   It seems to be particularly American, although also universal, that we deal with darkness and crisis in our lives by intense activity. Mary not only jumps to the "body-snatcher" conclusion, but she immediately springs into action. Forget the solemn attitude of mourning . She takes off running. We go places, we do things, and we speak up!

5/ We share our misconceptions with others. Mary is going to tell the others her conclusion and see what they can do together. What is it she "saith unto" Simon Peter? It's her theory – her eye-ball and general-experience conclusion (rather than an eyes-of-faith and spiritual-history conclusion.) "They have taken away the Lord out of the sepulchre." 'That's the way it looks to me.'

Again, we must be delicate when speaking negatively about sharing with others in the midst of trial and darkness. We're supposed to do that. "Bear one another's burdens and so fulfill the law of Christ." "Weep with those who weep and rejoice with those who rejoice." "Confess your sins to one another daily, lest you be hardened by the deceitfulness of sin." "Confess your sins and pray for one another that you may be healed." I would even go so far as to say it is better to go and tell someone else your own wrong conclusions about a crisis in your life than to keep it entirely to yourself. Another can often lead you when you are blind.

But as much wisdom as there may be in a multitude of counselors, the sum total of all our fleshly wisdom is zero. "Networking" with people, apart from faith and reliance on God's grace is something like the acerbic summary a friend gave me of how his business failed – "we were selling at a loss, but we tried to make it up in volume." Jesus is the way – he is the only way. No matter how big a crowd we may gather on any other road, we will not get an inch closer to understanding or to heaven.

A little saying that helps me strike the balance in these things (at least in theory) is this: God calls us not to independence of each other, nor to dependence on each other, but to interdependence with one another. We are independent only in relation to the world, the flesh and the devil. We are unilaterally dependent only in relation to God. But we are made and meant to be interdependent in relation to each other.

6/ We are deaf and blind to the comfort the Lord offers and unwilling to receive it. It is particularly striking here that Mary is oblivious to the nature of the two figures in the tomb. One can almost see her mind grinding away on her own pet theory of what has happened. She is so preoccupied with her feeble explanation, this effort to 'makes sense' of what she sees, that she doesn't see what's in front of her!

(Often people mock those who look beyond "what is seen," yet the mockers often fail to see even that. While disparaging those who are "so heavenly minded that they are no earthly good," those who are earthly minded are less earthly good!)

These beings are angels! These are bright celestial spirits mysteriously clad in a measure of visible glory and she takes them for casual bystanders who happen to be resting in the recently emptied tomb! We read elsewhere in the New Testament that we are to show hospitality to strangers for by doing so some have entertained angels unawares. Perhaps one devoted to ministering to others needs will not recognize angels in the joy of ministering to them, but in Mary's case their appearance is attended with plenty of divine fireworks. If the angels' natures are hidden from her, it is by her own preoccupation and unbelief.

In our times of trial, darkness and confusion we often tend to ask God for miraculous interventions. This passage may illustrate why he doesn't bother to send us miracles, or, when he does, we are not more often aware of them. A miraculous intervention, like any other act of God, requires a receptivity of faith. Eyes of unbelief never see a miracle – they always see something else.

The angels ask her "Why are you weeping?" The question is repeated again within a few verses. Weeping isn't always wrong. It's often to be recommended. But she is asked the question precisely because weeping isn't legitimate or appropriate here. Are we so lost in our own darknesses that we are unable to recognize and respond to a rescue party when God sends one?

The angels also ask, "Why do you seek the living among the dead?" That sounds like a pretty heavy hint to me. Yet I have ignored heavier ones in my time. Unbelief blinds us and stops our ears and minds. Like Puddleglum in C.S. Lewis' *The Silver Chair*, we find a perverse comfort in our gloomy perspectives.

As with Judas, the question is what kind of sorrow does our weeping indicate? Are we weeping in legitimate grief, which does not eclipse faith? Or is our sorrow worldly – a despairing and self-pitying idolatry? In my early teens I used to enjoy writing broken-hearted love songs – before I had any idea what that really meant – and quite enjoyed the "sweet sorrow" of singing them soulfully to myself. Is our sorrow, like that of some of the characters in another of C.S. Lewis's books, *The Great Divorce*, so deliciously self-indulgent that we don't want to be told we have less to mourn about than we thought?

7/ We don't recognize the object of our longing. Among useful things Christian counselors suggest is recognizing our longings are ultimately heavenly longings. When we do not recognize this we spend, indeed waste, a terrible amount of our lives seeking an elusive earthly fulfillment. Pure and simply put, Mary Magdalene longs for Jesus. The climax of this passage comes when Jesus himself appears behind her as she speaks with the angels, but she does not recognize him! He, too, asks her why she is weeping. He asks her whom she is seeking! Still she does not have a clue that it is he! And her blindness, like ours, takes her to the most ridiculous levels.

Thus far she has made two great errors about Jesus. First, she has concluded, apparently beyond a shadow of doubt, that he is dead. That error she shares with just about everyone. Second, she has concluded, with less evidence, that he is not only dead, but that his body has been stolen.

Now, we see her go on with two more errors – so foolish, and so much like us! She sees Jesus and thinks he is the gardener! And finally, she earnestly addresses him and begs him to reveal where he has hidden his own body. In other words, her fourth error is to conclude that he, himself, is the bodysnatcher!!!

We not only mistake the true circumstances when hardship appears in our lives, but we mistake the Lord for a fallible and even culpable agent of our supposed hardship! He has abandoned us! He has taken away those of his own good gifts that we need most! He has stolen himself from us!

8/ We have a plan that completely misses God's plan. At the sublime height of this divine comedy, Mary Magdalene proposes to Jesus that he give back the body he has stolen and stashed, in order that she may take it away – presumably to put it in some safe place, where it can be properly cared for!

Oh, Lord, how often you and the archangels must be reduced to helpless laughter over our extreme ability to get everything exactly backward. Perhaps your laughter is like Abraham Lincoln's during the Civil War, which he defended in these terms, "If I did not laugh, I would have to cry".

And we are able to look even more ridiculous than our sister Mary did -- for often we are devoted to that which is patently artificial and destructive. We mistake words and photos on paper and computer screens for passionate lovers. We purchase lottery lies as though they were tickets to heaven. We not only mistake you and accuse you, but we attempt emotional blackmail against you, and think we can force you into submission to us by threatening to go to hell instead of heaven. Lord forgive us – in the midst of your laughter and tears, forgive and change us.

The Mystery of Godliness

BUT In the midst of the still-dark times, something -- someone leads us, brings us, and ultimately speaks to us – contrary to what we "know" and "expect" and what we "naturally" do. What or who is it?

What brought Mary to the tomb? What kept her from going off and hiding or going back to the seven devils and the streets?

What brought Joseph of Arimathaea, the secret, fearful believer to identify himself with Christ at the point where all hope seemed to be lost?

What made John and Peter come running to the tomb? They knew not that he would rise. (John 20:9) In fact it seems to me John's "seeing and believing" in v.8 refers only to the fact that Jesus' body is missing as Mary had told them, since he goes on to say they did not know he must rise in v.9.

It is Jesus himself who meets us. God's grace is what keeps us going against all our inclinations "while it is yet dark". The Divine Comforter whom Jesus promised to send in full measure is the mysterious force that keeps up going despite all odds. The Holy Spirit not only intercedes for us with groans too deep for words, but he leads us through tough times with perseverance too deep for "good sense".

And what is it at last that "wakes us up"? What opens our eyes to the Lord? It is his gentle persistent presence saying our name (as he did Mary's) or breaking bread with us (as he did with the men on the road to Emmaus) or appearing in the midst of our mournful and fearful gatherings (as he did later that day with the disciples, and again in Galilee) or telling us to reach out and touch him in a way <u>custom-designed</u> <u>to</u> <u>assure</u> <u>us</u> (as he did later with Thomas).

Another of those threads of poetic power which run all through the scriptures may be seen in the juxtaposition of the three accounts we have of Jesus around tombs. In one, he calls the name "Lazarus" and his friend stumbles out, still wrapped in grave clothes. In yet another, he asks a demon-possessed man what his name is. (Or perhaps it would be more accurate to say he demands the demons tell their names, in order to cast them out so the true man can again emerge under his true name.) (Luke 8:30) In another, he says "Mary" and suddenly a worried and despairing woman is filled with faith and joy.

In both the other recorded cases where he raises the dead he addresses them directly: "Young man, I say unto thee, Arise" (Luke 7:14) and "Talitha, cumi" ('Maiden, get up') just after the Gadarene demoniac, in Luke 8:54. The results of Jesus speaking to us - calling us by name or demanding that we render up our true spiritual identity and allegiance, at least in the cases cited -- is to raise the dead, restore one to his right mind, give faith and comfort, and to restore life. When Jesus speaks to us, addresses us by name, it is revolutionary. And Jesus does speak to us in the dark times as he did to these.

Nevertheless, our little hearts and little minds find it hard to keep on while it is "yet dark". Things often seem permanently dark to us when in fact there are miracles ready to happen. Like the disciples right before the feeding of the five thousand, we are ready to help the Lord out by telling him how dark things are: "Lord this is a desert place and the time is far gone." (Matthew 14:15) —'Lord, the pickings are scarce and it's getting late! Send 'em all home'. 'Let us go home, too, Lord. Let's give up on this losing proposition.'

But the Lord will reveal himself. Growing in faith can be measured in many ways -- one way is according to the length of time we persevere between sightings!

Jesus himself went through a number of parallel experiences - culminating in a penultimate time of confusion, agony, dread in the Garden of Gethsemane. There it was "yet dark" for him in a way we cannot know, for he anticipated our hell and agreed to take the weight of our sin.

Then he willingly entered into the ultimate trial, the darkest darkness any man shall ever know – taking that weight indeed to the full crushing of himself. "My God, my God, why hast thou forsaken me!" was not a cry of denial, not a failure to recognize, but a cry of faith continuing beyond that awful point where Jesus was separated from the Father by our sins. He has indeed been tempted in all ways like unto us -- and beyond us -- yet without sin.

The Lord will give us grace at least as great as that given Mary Magdalene and the disciples during this dark time. He will give us grace to:

- Still say no to sin when we can't remember exactly why.
- Still speak gently to the members of our family when they clearly need to be kicked.
- Still get together and hang together with other Christians although they are such peculiar people -- with more problems than solutions.
- Wait and persevere through loss, through pain, and through a feeling of loneliness or abandonment.

And we fail – we will fail – we will sin. But the Lord says "Mary" or "Bill" or "Sue" or "Tom" or "Joan" or "Jim" and our hearts are suddenly full with recognition – MY LORD! MY SAVIOR! MY RISEN JESUS! How did I miss you! How could I mistake you! Now I see, now I know! Now I will rejoice! The darkness has vanished and you are my light.

Chapter Seven: Conspiracy Theories

– The Pharisees' "conspiracy theory" parallel to
Mary and disciples': both versus the genuine conspiracy

Matthew 27:62-66
62 Now the next day, that followed the day of preparation, the chief priests and Pharisees came together unto Pilate,
63 Saying, Sir, we remember that that deceiver said, while he was yet alive, After three days I will rise again.
64 Command therefore that the sepulchre be made sure until the third day, lest his disciples come by night, and steal him away, and say unto the people, He is risen from the dead: so the last error shall be worse than the first.
65 Pilate said unto them, Ye have a watch: go your way, make it as sure as ye can.
66 So they went, and made the sepulchre sure, sealing the stone, and setting a watch.

Matthew 28:2-4
2 And, behold, there was a great earthquake: for the angel of the Lord descended from heaven, and came and rolled back the stone from the door, and sat upon it.
3 His countenance was like lightning, and his raiment white as snow:
4 And for fear of him the keepers did shake, and became as dead men.

John 20: 2, 8, 13, 15
2 Then she runneth, and cometh to Simon Peter, and to the other disciple, whom Jesus loved, and saith unto them, They have taken away the Lord out of the sepulcher, and we know not where they have laid him.
. . .
8 Then went in also that other disciple, which came first to the sepulchre, and he saw, and believed.
. . .
13 And they say unto her, Woman, why weepest thou? She saith unto them, Because they have taken away my Lord, and I know not where they have laid him.

. . .

15 Jesus saith unto her, Woman, why weepest thou? Whom seekest thou? She, supposing him to be the gardener, saith unto him, Sir, if thou have borne him hence, tell me where thou hast laid him, and I will take him away.

Matthew 28:11-15
11 Now when they [the women] were going, behold, some of the watch came into the city, and shewed unto the priests all the things that were done.
12 And when they were assembled with the elders, and had taken counsel, they gave large money unto the soldiers,
13 Saying, Say ye, His disciples came by night, and stole him away while we slept.
14 And if this come to the governor's ears, we will persuade him, and secure you.
15 So they took the money, and did as they were taught: and this saying is commonly reported among the Jews until this day.

For all my picking on Mary Magdalene in the last chapter, I hope we agreed together that Jesus is the one who kept her, who keeps us even while it is yet dark. I also hope we agree together in the joy that rises in our hearts as we meditate on the resurrection. It is like a good yeast that raises a loaf overnight, ready to be baked into a tall and golden offering -- too good to eat. It is like the stir in every heart at a wedding when the bride comes down the aisle. It is like the wonder of a circus where the crazy clown attempts some horribly dangerous act, and is suddenly revealed to us as an accomplished acrobat. In short, we cannot remain unexcited or somber. The resurrection of Christ has brought a divine hilarity into history.

At this point in the narratives we may become so light-hearted than we cannot take anything too seriously. We may incline to see the remainder as the merely a denouement, a wrapping up of loose ends. But let us see it through to the end – and laugh new-naturedly at ourselves, while we rejoice to the roots of our beings.

The conspiracy theme recurs. As we mentioned before, Mary Magdalene jumped quickly to the wrong conclusion and told others that "they" took the body, "they" caused her troubles, and even "you" when she thought Jesus was the gardener- 'the fault lies with someone else' – in the same way as Adam was sure the source of his problems was "the woman you gave me".

At Mary Magdalene's urging Peter and John ran to see. The scripture tells us "they believed". Does this mean they believed Christ had risen, or rather that they joined her in believing a conspiracy theory -- agreeing that "they" had taken the body. I think it is the latter. My strongest arguments for this are: first, the verse subsequent to the one that tells us they believed also says they did not yet understand the scripture that he must rise. (John 20:9) Second the same verb "believe" is used in John 19, verse 35:

> 34 But one of the soldiers with a spear pierced his side, and forthwith came there out blood and water.
> 35 And he that saw it bare record, and his record is true; and he knoweth that he saith true, that ye might believe.

Here "believe" almost certainly means "accept the particular evidence (that Jesus really died) as true". (At one step removed, of course, these passages may also imply "believe in the resurrected Jesus".)

If mine is the correct interpretation of "believed," then John and Peter agreed to the conspiracy theory of body-snatching which Mary proposed. It is quite likely, in fact, that when she suggested it they were predisposed to agree, being inclined to nourish small fears into greater fears with only a little fodder.

But look who else has formulated a conspiracy theory! The Pharisees, too, suspect body-snatchers! And we must give them credit for better memories than the disciples. Their basis for suspecting a conspiracy is the memory of Jesus' prophecies

47.

of his own resurrection. This, in fact, seems to be the first account we have of a right interpretation of the somewhat mysterious predictions he made on the subject.

So the Pharisees, being both better at remembering and more forward-thinking than the disciples, send and request that Pilate have the tomb guarded. Pilate sends a detachment of his soldiers. (I think these are his soldiers, perhaps someone more knowledgeable would say they were the temple guards. On the face of it that would seem less likely given the subsequent necessity of bribing them with lots of money.) They seal the stone and set a watch.

The problem with the Pharisees' conspiracy theory is not that there wasn't one, but that, like Mary, they had the wrong conspirators in mind. When the earth's elements join with the angels of God, lowest and the highest creatures, in a conspiracy to break open the tomb; and when the Lord himself, by the Holy Spirit, breaks out, it is far more than they bargained for. One hopes at least one of their own representatives, left behind to make sure the soldiers did not slip up, was among those who "became as dead men" out of sheer fright at the trembling of the ground, the lightning-like appearance of the angels, and the rolling back of the stone. It is an argument from silence, but since they did not call the soldiers liars when these events were reported, it may be one or two of them were indeed at the scene.

After this Mary, who seems by some accounts to have seen the cataclysms, heavenly messengers, et cetera, (but perhaps she too became for a time as a dead man), runs to the apostles with her body-snatcher tale – and persists in holding to it during her subsequent conversations with the angels and with Jesus himself. (At least she is right in the end – he <u>has</u> in an ultimate sense snatched his own body from the grave, if not in the person of a gardener!)

The sad and pathetic end of the conspiracy approach to the resurrection comes in the Pharisee's further deceit. Here we see the bargain with the devil played out in all its Faustian pathos. The Pharisees enter fully into the hypocrisy of doing the very things of which they have hotly accused their enemies – the Pharisees <u>do</u> become conspirators.

Not that they haven't carried on a sort of conspiracy already, but now the last of their excuses for it is gone. They have the testimony of the guards at the tomb. The guards must have told the Pharisees what had happened to the best of their catatonic memories, after which the Pharisees immediately conferred and bribed the witnesses that they might commit perjury in regard to the facts. (This may have also involved a species of blackmail – for as military men, they had technically fallen asleep at their posts – a potentially capital offense.)

The final poetic touch is this: their cooked-up testimony was to be that the conspiracy the Pharisees feared had come true, that the very thing which the guards were assigned to prevent had taken place. Somehow someone had got past the guards, rolled away the stone, and sneaked away with Jesus' body. As for possible repercussions to the guards, the Pharisees vowed they would use all their influence to make sure there weren't any.

Conspiracy theories are ways of defining ourselves negatively. Bitter political polarizations, regional and racial feuds – family schisms and church splits all grow out of unbelief and the fear of man. If Jesus is at the center of our lives and we know him to be the Savior and Son of the Sovereign God, we do not fear men "whose breath is in their nostrils". We do not fear men who are like the flowering grass, who flourish today and tomorrow wither. We do not fear those who can kill the body, but rather Him who can cast both body and soul into hell. Holding to conspiracy theories is sure evidence of a little faith and a little god.

When men approach the resurrection they have a choice: between entering fully into the fear of God which it inspires; or denying him and conspiring against him in the face of truth and high fact.

Therefore it is a particularly sad testimony that conspiracy theories and those who profit from them are so common in the American Christian church. It is certainly true that there is a kingdom of darkness and that it seems to be exercising tremendous sway over the laws and mores of our society. It is true that abortion is a terrible evil and that euthanasia follows swiftly on its heels. But it is not true that God has human enemies with a world-wide web of power, nor that collectively the slaves of darkness (for that is what they all are, as we all once were – slaves, not masters) have power enough to rival God. We can effectively stand against specific evil in specific times and places by faith, but are hindered from doing so when we concoct and jabber about conspiracy theories. We can only focus on one thing at a time – and when we begin to focus on the machinations of God's enemies, we cease focusing on our conquering Lord.

We indeed have an enemy, but his power was broken by the very events we discuss. He is still active, but he is losing. Ironically, conspiracy theories in the church are one of the devil's tactics. They keep us busy on non-essentials, instead of repenting in areas where our own idolatries are among the things reinforcing the evils we're blaming on various conspiracies.

Chapter Eight: Slow Of Heart

– Road to Emmaus

Mark 16:11-13
11 And they [the disciples], when they had heard that he was alive, and had been seen of her [Mary Magdalene], believed not.
12 After that he appeared in another form unto two of them, as they walked, and went into the country.
13 And they went and told it unto the residue: neither believed they them.

Luke 24:13-35
[On the first day of the week – when Mary, Peter and John had been to the tomb]
13 And, behold, two of them went that same day to a village called Emmaus, which was from Jerusalem about threescore furlongs.
14 And they talked together of all these things which had happened.
15 And it came to pass, that, while they communed together and reasoned, Jesus himself drew near, and went with them.
16 But their eyes were holden that they should not know him.
17 And he said unto them, What manner of communications are these that ye have one to another, as ye walk, and are sad?
18 And the one of them, whose name was Cleopas, answering said unto him, Art thou only a stranger in Jerusalem, and hast not known the things which are come to pass there in these days?
19 And he said unto them, What things? And they said unto him, Concerning Jesus of Nazareth, which was a prophet mighty in deed and word before God and all the people:
20 And how the chief priests and our rulers delivered him to be condemned to death, and have crucified him.
21 But we trusted that it had been he which should have redeemed Israel: and beside all this, today is the third day since these things were done.
22 Yea, and certain women also of our company made us astonished, which were early at the sepulchre;
23 And when they found not his body, they came, saying, that they had also seen a vision of angels, which said that he was alive.
24 And certain of them which were with us went to the sepulchre, and found it even so as the women had said: but him they saw not.

25 Then he said to them, O fools, and slow of heart to believe all that the prophets have spoken:
26 Ought not the Christ to have suffered these things, and to enter into his glory?
27 And beginning at Moses and all the prophets, he expounded unto them in all the scriptures the things concerning himself.
28 And they drew nigh unto the village, whither they went: and he made as though he would have gone further.
29 But they constrained him, saying, Abide with us: for it is toward evening, and the day is far spent. And he went in to tarry with them.
30 And it came to pass, as he sat at meat with them, he took bread, and blessed it, and brake, and gave to them.
31 And their eyes were opened, and they knew him; and he vanished out of their sight.
32 And they said one to another, Did not our hearts burn within us, while he talked with us by the way, and while he opened to us the scriptures?
33 And they rose up the same hour, and returned to Jerusalem, and found the eleven gathered together, and them that were with them,
34 Saying, The Lord is risen indeed, and hath appeared to Simon.
35 And they told what things were done in the way, and how he was known to them in breaking of bread.

This wonderful episode in the post-resurrection account stirs us to that ebullience we spoke of earlier – an overflowing of joy that makes us both light-hearted and filled with awe – in sympathy with those two men who traveled toward Emmaus.

But Jesus direct words in the story express one of its strongest themes – "O fools, and slow of heart to believe all that the prophets have spoken." Notice that the disciples did not believe Mary Magdalene when she told them she had seen the Lord. Yet they hadn't any problem believing her earlier conspiracy theory! O fools, and slow of heart! Notice that the disciples did not believe the other women, either. Oh fools and slow of heart! Notice that these two men do not express, even as bare theory, a faith or expectation that Jesus might indeed be risen. Oh fools, and slow of heart! And notice that when they take their account back to the disciples, among whom Peter also has seen the risen Lord (an account of which meeting we do not have), these two are also disbelieved.

After the resurrection the two strands or themes are 1/the evidence, and 2/the foolishness and slowness of our hearts to believe. Everyone of my children has experienced that classic childhood mini-drama, in which Mom or Dad tells you something which sounds to you unlikely and difficult to believe. The time comes to mind when my oldest daughter, Kimiko, and I walked along a path beside Tookany Creek not far from our home in Philadelphia. "Be careful, Kimi. Don't touch this plant, because it will give you an ouch. It's called nettles and if you touch it, it makes your skin feel like its burning." Less than a minute later I heard her voice behind me sobbing. You know what happened. Yet I have touched nettles a thousand times since, and far worse ones than those that merely burn your skin. Oh Lord, deliver us foolish and slow of heart to believe!

The account of Jesus meeting and walking and talking and consenting to stay with the two travelers is so wonderful that one hardly knows where to begin. It is one of those accounts which hides nothing, but contains more than can be explored or exposited. It is one of those passages that one can soak in, like a hot bath.

It is not at Jesus' rebuke, nor in Jesus' explanation of the scriptures that they recognize him, but rather it is in the breaking of the bread. No matter what our theology of the Lord's Table may be, none of us can afford to discount or deflate its precious nature. It is a sacrament of recognition, and one we cannot afford to be without. At the same time it is a memorial and promise of being together – first with Jesus and then with each other. We need to recognize him again and again. When he gathered together with his disciples before he went to the cross (as they scattered) he gave us the sacrament and told us to do this "in remembrance of me". That was because he knows us – forgetful, foolish, and slow of heart to believe. He also promised to eat and drink it again with us in heaven. But it is something more, and the great error of all our wrangling is that "both sides" seem to explain away the mystery of it.

It was as they showed him hospitality that Jesus was revealed to them. My friend Richard Wyatt told me it is said of Robert Bridges that he once asked Gerard Manley Hopkins how he could be sure about the things of the Christian faith, to which Hopkins replied, "give alms". Jesus seems to have said something very similar in Matthew 25: Inasmuch as ye have done it unto one of the least of these my brethren, ye have done it unto me. It is chilling to note that he states the converse, too – that as often as we haven't done it unto the least of these, we do it not unto him – and further, that all this is intimately tied up with judgment, the separation of the blessed into the Father's kingdom and the cursed into everlasting punishment.

Another wonderful parallel – indeed one that climaxes in the reading of that very scripture passage – is the story (originally by Tolstoy, it was also adapted into a Christmas play and movie, and a Clay-mation movie) about the old shoemaker, Martin, who dreams of Christ visiting him, but is unsure if He will indeed come. He has several opportunities during the day to help needy people in ways that seem to him inconsequential. In the conclusion of the Christmas movie version, his sceptical friend stands by as a priest happens in that evening and begins to read Matthew 25 to him. Both dismiss the pastor, but the sceptic picks up the Bible and reads on. Suddenly it comes home to them – the Lord Jesus has answered the shoemaker's prayer and come to him – in the form of those "least" brethren.

Jesus is recognized in the breaking of bread and in serving the least of these his brethren. We cannot neglect either.

SECTION II : LAST APPEARANCES

-- After the Resurrection is Revealed

According to the first chapter of Acts, there were forty days between Jesus resurrection and his ascension. But there is no neat delineation between the post-crucifixion/pre-resurrection struggles of the disciples and the post-resurrection/pre-ascension narratives. Might we go further and say there is no sharp distinction between the post-resurrection/pre-ascension church and the present post-ascension/pre-return church. Christ's work was finished on the cross, the certainty of our justification was manifested on earth and sealed in heaven at that time. However, the resurrection was the evidence and declaration Christ's work was finished, while the applying of that work to our lives continues. Each of us comes to trust in Christ. Each of us is transformed more and more into his image (the process part of sanctification). If that's too much theology or at least too many four syllable words to take in, the main point is that we can "relate" to the baby church's struggles because they are pretty much the same as ours.

There is some overlap with passages we have already discussed in these final four chapters – but we will not cover that ground again. If there is any change from what has gone before it is this: now the church is entering into a fuller sense of what it believes and what its Head has done. Nonetheless, the struggle of faith continues.

When It Was Yet Dark

Chapter Nine: Gathering For Gloom And Glory

-- The Upper Room

Mark 16:14-18

14 Afterward he appeared unto the eleven as they sat at meat, and upbraided them with their unbelief and hardness of heart, because they believed not them which had seen him after he was risen.

15 And he said unto them, Go ye into all the world, and preach the gospel to every creature.

16 He that believeth and is baptized shall be saved; but he that believeth not shall be damned.

17 And these signs shall follow them that believe; In my name shall they cast out devils; they shall speak with new tongues;

18 They shall take up serpents; and if they drink any deadly thing, it shall not hurt them; they shall lay hands on the sick, and they shall recover.

Luke 24:35-36, 44-49

35 And they [the two men on the road to Emmaus] told what things were done in the way, and how he was known of them in breaking of bread.

36 And as they thus spake, Jesus himself stood in the midst of them, and saith unto them, Peace be unto you.

37 But they were terrified and affrighted, and supposed that they had seen a spirit.

. . .

44 And he said unto them, These are the words which I spake unto you, while I was yet with you, that all things must be fulfilled, which were written in the law of Moses, and in the prophets, and in the psalms, concerning me.

45 Then opened he their understanding, that they might understand the scriptures,

46 And said unto them, Thus it is written, and thus it behooved Christ to suffer, and to rise from the dead the third day:

47 And that repentance and remission of sins should be preached in his name among all nations, beginning at Jerusalem.

48 And ye are witnesses of these things.

49 And, behold, I send the promise of my Father upon you: but tarry ye in the city of Jerusalem until ye be endued with power from on high.

John 20:19-23
[the first day of the week in which Mary saw Jesus near the tomb]
19 Then the same day at evening, being the first day of the week, when the doors were shut where the disciples were assembled for fear of the Jews, came Jesus and stood in the midst, and saith unto them, Peace be unto you.
20 And when he had so said, he shewed unto them his hands and his side. Then were the disciples glad, when they saw the Lord.
21 Then said Jesus to them again, Peace be unto you: as my Father hath sent me, even so send I you.
22 And when he had said this, he breathed on them, and saith unto them, Receive the Holy Ghost:
23 Whose soever sins ye remit, they are remitted unto them; and whose soever sins ye retain, they are retained.

The list of witnesses to the resurrection has grown long, but the most important credibility barrier has not been breached. The centurion and crowd at the cross testified to some measure of divinity in Jesus; Mary and the women at the tomb testified to his resurrection; the two on the road to Emmaus brought a similar report, but the "church," that is this core group of motley leaders, is still skeptical. (Historically this is but the first instance of something that is almost a rule: church leadership is often the last to catch on to what the Lord is doing.) But then, even as the two from the Emmaus road tell their story, Jesus appears to the gathered group. In the words of Don Francisco's wonderful song ("He's Alive") "Suddenly the room was filled with strange and sweet perfume." Jesus stood among them.

Jesus first comforts them ("Peace be with you") and assures them, for they thought he was a disembodied spirit of some kind. Therefore he demonstrates he is physically risen from the grave. He rebukes them for their hardness of heart as he did the two on Emmaus road. Also, as he did on that occasion, he opens the scriptures for them explaining how he had to suffer and to rise on the third day.

Jesus stood among them, and all but Thomas were brought on board as witnesses. He comes to them when they are together -- so that the testimony is now unassailable so far as the church is concerned. On the other hand, there really hasn't been a church until now. As the risen Christ appears, the church is formed. A Universal Council has now witnessed his resurrection and has agreed to it. Further affirmations hereafter have to do with the conversion of individuals. The debate about the resurrection (versus body-snatching) is over. The church of Christ will never open it again.

But there is much more going on, now that the "witness" phase of the story is over. In a real sense, the church has just been reborn, and immediately, we read, she gets her commission. She has gotten her commission before in various seminal forms ever since creation and at various phases of the history of Israel. She will get it again, apparently, to the extent we can decipher the chronology of these gospel passages. But here we get, for the first time, what we take to be the abiding formula which will stand until the world ends and the Lord returns. We are to go into the whole world and preach the gospel. We are to preach repentance and the remission of sins. We are to preach it to every creature. We are in some nearly-incredible sense to oversee the remission of sins and the condemnation of those who do not heed the gospel we preach. But the church is not quite ready to take off on this mission. Jesus says wait -- there remains an important promise of the Father which is yet to be fulfilled in you.

Jesus breathes on them -- a new creation story seems to be taking place, for so God breathed on the lump of clay which became Adam at the very beginning. (Is this not the same breath they thought had gone forever when it stopped on the cross!) He says he is sending them out in the same way the Father sent him into the world. (There is a rich irony in "Peace be unto you: as my Father hath sent me, even so send I you." It reminds me of the words of a modern hymn, "The peace of God it is no peace, but strife closed in the sod, yet brothers pray for just one thing, the marvelous peace of God.") Jesus tells them they are to have powerful signs accompanying them, affirming the witness of their preaching. But he says 'Wait. There is yet a promise of the Father -- there is yet a promise to be fulfilled of power coming upon you from on high.'

I am neither a Pentecostal nor a Charismatic as most would define those labels. I believe that in the same way as the Crucifixion and Resurrection were particular events not to be repeated, so was the imminent pouring out of the Holy Spirit at Pentecost. But I am strongly of the opinion that there is a paradigm and pattern in these passages for Christian obedience.

It is one thing to get the facts right (Christ is risen). It is another thing to receive a commission (go into all the world and preach the gospel to all creatures). But something far beyond facts and instructions to repeat them is required of us. We must wait for God's timing, God's power and presence -- or we "understand" and "go" in vain.

The Christian church has floundered again and again through the error of thinking that dogma plus duty made a commission. We will end up waiting one way or another -- either beforehand on our knees or a little later on our faces. We need the Holy Spirit to do the holy work.

Chapter Ten: Faith and The Five Senses

– Touch me not. Touch me.

John 20:16-18

16 Jesus saith unto her, Mary. She turned herself, and saith unto him, Rabboni; which is to say, Master.

17 Jesus saith unto her, Touch me not; for I am not yet ascended to my Father: but go to my brethren, and say unto them, I ascend unto my Father, and your Father; and to my God, and your God.

18 Mary Magdalene came and told the disciples that she had seen the Lord, and that he had spoken these things unto her.

Matthew 28:8-10

8 And they [the women] departed quickly from the sepulchre with fear and great joy; and did run to bring his disciples word.

9 And as they went to tell his disciples, behold, Jesus met them, saying, All hail. And they came and held him by the feet, and worshipped him.

10 Then said Jesus unto them, Be not afraid: go tell my brethren that they go into Galilee, and there shall they see me.

Luke 24:37-43

37 But they [the disciples in the Upper Room] were terrified and affrighted, and supposed that they had seen a spirit.

38 And he said unto them, Why are ye troubled? And why do thoughts arise in your hearts?

39 Behold my hands and my feet, that it is I myself, handle me, and see, for a spirit hath not flesh and bones, as ye see me have.

40 And when he had thus spoken, he shewed them his hands and his feet.

41 And while they yet believed not for joy, and wondered, he said unto them, Have ye here any meat?

42 And they gave him a piece of a broiled fish, and of an honeycomb.

43 And he took it, and did eat before them.

John 20:20, 24-31

20 And when he had so said, he shewed unto them his hands and his side. Then were the disciples glad, when they saw the Lord.

. . .

24 But Thomas, one of the twelve, called Didymus, was not with them when Jesus came.

25 The other disciples therefore said unto him, We have seen the Lord. But he said unto them, Except I shall see in his hands the print of the nails, and put my finger into the print of the nails, and thrust my hand into his side, I will not believe.

26 And after eight days again his disciples were within, and Thomas with them: then came Jesus, the doors being shut, and stood in the midst, and said, Peace be unto you.

27 Then saith he to Thomas, reach hither thy finger, and behold my hands; and reach hither thy hand, and thrust it into my side: and be not faithless but believing.

28 And Thomas answered and said unto him, My Lord and my God.

29 Jesus saith unto him, Thomas, because thou has seen me, thou hast believed: blessed are they that have not seen, and yet have believed.

30 And many other signs truly did Jesus in the presence of his disciples, which are not written in this book:

31 But these are written, that ye might believe that Jesus is the Christ, the Son of God; and that believing ye might have life through his name.

Why did Jesus tell Mary not to touch him, yet soon thereafter allows the women to embrace his feet? Why does he direct Thomas to touch him when seeing him surely would have been enough?

The natural tendency for us is to look for explanations that diffuse the mystery surrounding the resurrection events or at least make it less mysterious to us. We've had the spirits of the dead wandering around amidst earthquakes and eclipses; we've had temple veils ripping down the middle from top to bottom; we've had hardened soldiers struck dumb at the lightning-like appearances of angels rolling the stone from the grave. And so on.

The funny thing is that the "explanations" we come up with for these supernatural events are always pretty "naturalistic". We tend to think Jesus told Mary not to touch him in the same way one puts a sign on a freshly painted door, "Wet Paint"! Or that he told Thomas to touch him because Thomas needed the tactile in order to believe.

These things are happening, however in the context of the church's founding. The central issue of her founding – as of her continuing – is always faith. Both Mary and Thomas show us dimensions of unbelief, which is the greatest sin within this new entity. As Jesus deals with them we are shown the opposite -- what it looks like to come to faith. And again in Jesus' particular word to each of them, we are told some important things about faith's opponent.

When Jesus tells Mary not to touch him, contrary to our instinctive interpretations, it can hardly be because there is some supernatural necessity that he be "fixed": or "sealed" before he can properly be touched. The "going to the Father," the Ascension, is not to occur for forty days. We can scarcely imagine what kind of "reunion" took place between the risen Son and the Father immediately upon the completion of the atonement for sin, but certainly this eternal "reunion" began before Jesus revealed himself to Mary Magdalene, and of course, it continues never broken again forever. -- We wander into areas of mystery too profound for us. Even my attempts to maintain mystery here are too rational. Perhaps in heaven we will be able to ask appropriate questions about them.

A more profitable and I think much more suitable discussion finds it focus in what Jesus tells Mary: 1/that he's got things to do, and 2/ that she's got a few things to do, too. In other words, much as it was at the Mount of Transfiguration, ' C'mon, let's get busy. No, we can't stop here, now. We've all got tasks to do.'

That he would meet Mary and the other women even as they were carrying the all-important message to the disciples -- and there allow them the further blessing of embracing his crucified and risen feet may be interpreted both on and beyond the simply literal. Does it not illustrate that the greatest intimacies we experience with the Lord occur as we are in the midst of his business?

At another level throughout these passages there is a contrast between evidence and faith: the five senses versus spiritual perception. Mary has trusted her senses and reason too much up to this point, and they have failed her miserably, so that she did not even recognize Jesus when she saw and heard him. Now she wishes to worship him with her senses, perhaps by falling at his feet and embracing him. He says no: 'worship me with spiritual service and by bearing a message (as a witness) from yours to my disciples' hearts.'

He does not discourage her senses and embraces as though they are in themselves bad. The embraces later that day (perhaps later that morning) are welcomed and received. The physical is emphasized when Jesus comes to the upper room -- for the disciples like Mary have not been able to believe without any "evidence" to their five senses. There is a rebuke, a reference to hardness of heart. And Thomas, the last to believe, becomes the epitome of this whole new lesson, complete with its formulation.

Adam's sin, and Eve's temptation took place through an appeal to their spirits through the five senses. They responded to the serpent's spiritual appeal through their senses, despite the reality of walking and talking with God in the Garden in an intimacy which was "whole," that is both spiritual and physical. (Including his provision of all, their own physical intimacy, their unashamed bodily nakedness, et cetera.) This intimacy was broken through a denial of one part in favor of an appeal to the other. The apple looked good, they imagined it would taste good. The serpent said it would give (spiritual) knowledge of good and evil (knowledge without experience -- such as God alone can have), and the act itself involved "tasting," trying with the (physical) senses. That is a very brief and inadequate attempt to describe the incredible complex of spiritual dynamics going on in the Fall! But my point is that we can look at Thomas now and hear Jesus' words to him, in light of the full picture of redemption.

Jesus is saying, 'I know you rely on your senses as aids to believe. You think you need evidence. I will condescend to that. Come and get it.' Just as he spoke Mary's name, allowing her the aural in addition to the visual evidence, rather than standing silently waiting (forever?) for her to recognize him, so he bends himself, and humbles himself, uncovering and offering his wounds to Thomas, visually and tactilely, so that Thomas, too, can believe. (Shakespeare's genius in *Coriolanus* is showing us a "hero" quite the opposite -- too proud to display his wounds.)

At the point where Thomas suddenly realizes the enormity of his unbelieving "demands," the Lord affirms them as the divine blueprint according to which Thomas must come to him. Thomas is properly humiliated (brought low, literally to the dirt, or perhaps to face the dust of Adam in him) through being commanded to do exactly what he demanded he be allowed to do. His foolishness becomes the route for God's mercy.

It seems to me this has two levels of application. First, the Lord often does the same with us. We make the most ridiculous demands of him, and as he convicts us of how wrong we are, he proceeds to transform our demands into his benevolence. Second, and most central to this passage, the Lord is setting the church up to a full realization of the point referred to above: that she needs more than just the facts of the resurrection, and the "duty" of the great commission. She needs that power from on high in order to believe.

The church is to go forward on the basis of a "sense" which leads to faith, but it is to be the most ineffable of senses – hearing. Not seeing, which is described in antithesis to faith; not feeling, which is the most intimate and concrete of the senses, not even by tasting or smelling, which at least seem to give substantial evidence of a concrete corresponding reality. Hearing – and not even hearing of the immediate object – not the voice of God or the singing of angels, but hearing of the preaching, speaking, mumbling of the gospel. That is how faith is to come!

Jesus makes Thomas go through with what must have seemed a humiliation, and further seals it with the exhortation, "be not faithless but believing." Thomas is only the latest of a series of unbelieving and hard-hearted disciples, but he comes in for the toughest treatment, partly at least, because he has

65.

held out the longest -- against the testimony of the whole church. On the other hand, every one of the others has been given the evidence of their senses, so that he is no worse than they.

Thomas replies with a solid profession, "My Lord and My God"! But then Jesus goes on to teach what is the main import of this narrative, and it is a lesson that applies to every one there, no less than to Thomas, "Thomas, because thou has seen me, thou hast believed: blessed are they that have not seen, and yet have believed."

The Holy Spirit is to be poured out -- and by that Spirit, men and women will become able to believe without seeing. They will be able to hear and believe the testimony of the church. They will have better eyes to see the Lord and better fingers to feel his wounds. They will be able to hear this testimony and read it and hear it read, and know by these scriptures that Jesus is indeed the risen Lord and Savior. I believe the Holy Spirit was poured out in his fullness once and for all at Pentecost, but Jesus has already given the disciples the Spirit in some measure when he breathed on them and said "receive ye the Holy Spirit." (John 20:22) Without the Spirit, all the evidence in the world would not have made Mary or Thomas believe – or kept them believing.

The signs and wonders require the further affirmation of the Holy Spirit's testimony within us. But the signs and wonders were given us as "pegs" upon which the Holy Spirit hangs that affirmation. Thus John the gospel-writer concludes:

> And many other signs truly did Jesus in the presence of his disciples, which are not written in this book: But these are written, that ye might believe that Jesus is the Christ, the Son of God; and that believing ye might have life through his name. (John 20:30-31)

Notice also, that, with evidence given to their eyes and even to their touch, the disciples are yet unbelieving. "They believed not for joy, and wondered. . ." – it is too wonderful a thing to believe. Often we hold back for fear something is too good to be true. It is one thing to doubt what our eyes can't see or what seems contrary to what we have seen – but when we see something that is the very essence of our deepest longing – we don't believe then either! Our senses are not enough. Faith is a gift. We cannot believe unless the Lord gives us the gift, but he does. And like a patient mother or father, he works with us in the midst of our fears and failings. When the disciples believed not "for joy," he gave them grace and the further demonstration of his physical resurrection by eating something. There is continual divine condescension to our childish natures.

Lord, meet us in the fulfillment of our longings in you, and with the patient ministry of your Holy Spirit that we may believe, and believe more.

One further application: the Thomas passage shows us something about how to love sinners. I mentioned *Coriolanus*, earlier, in which the main character is a king who falls from power largely because he will not humble himself. This is sharply epitomized in his refusal to show the scars of his battle wounds in public – to allow the "hoi-poloi" to see and feel them. There is no reason to think the crowd had "the right" to see his scars, anymore than Thomas had the "right" to see those of Jesus. In the same way, people often want us to humble ourselves in relation to them. Others may not have "the right" to demand things of us, but it may nevertheless be right for us to "go the second mile" or "turn the other cheek", or 'show them our scars'. In refusing to "lower" ourselves to meet sinners where they are, we may commit the sin of demanding "our right" to personal privacy and dignity – a demand which Jesus alone could have made – and one which he did not. Coriolanus is a tragic hero and a useful reminder.

When It Was Yet Dark

Chapter Eleven: Gone Fishing

-- Galilean retreat

Mark 14:27-28
27 And Jesus saith unto them, All ye shall be offended because of me this night: for it is written, I shall smite the shepherd and the sheep will be scattered [see Zechariah 13:7]
28 But after that I am risen, I will go before you into Galilee.

Matthew 28:10
10 Then said Jesus unto them, Be not afraid: go tell my brethren that they go into Galilee, and there shall they see me.

Matthew 28:16-17
16 Then the eleven disciples went away into Galilee, into a mountain where Jesus had appointed them.
17 And when they saw him, they worshipped him, but some doubted.

John 21:1-19
1 After these things Jesus showed himself again to the disciples at the Sea of Tiberias; and on this wise showed he himself.
2 There were together Simon Peter, and Thomas called Didymus, and Nathaniel of Cana in Galilee, and the sons of Zebedee, and two other of his disciples.
3 Simon Peter saith unto them, I go a fishing. They say unto him, We also go with thee. They went forth, and entered into a ship immediately; and that night they caught nothing.
4 But when morning was now come, Jesus stood on the shore: but the disciples knew not that it was Jesus.
5 Then Jesus saith unto them, Children, have ye any meat? They answered him, No.
6 And he said unto them, Cast the net on the right side of the ship, and ye shall find. They cast therefore, and now they were not able to draw it for the multitude of fishes.
7 Therefore that disciple whom Jesus loved saith unto Peter, It is the Lord. Now when Simon Peter heard that it was the Lord, he girt his fishers coat unto him, (for he was naked,) and did cast himself into the sea.

8 And the other disciples came in a little ship; (for they were not far from land, but as it were two hundred cubits,) dragging the net with fishes.
9 As soon then as they were come to land, they saw a fire of coals there, and fish laid thereon and bread.
10 Jesus saith unto them, Bring of the fish which ye have caught.
11 Simon Peter went up and drew the net to land full of great fishes, a hundred and fifty and three: and for all there were so many, yet was not the net broken.
12 Jesus saith unto them, Come and dine. And none of the disciples durst ask him, Who art thou? Knowing that it was the Lord.
13 Jesus then cometh, and taketh bread, and giveth them, and fish likewise.
14 This is now the third time that Jesus showed himself to his disciples, after that he was risen from the dead.
15 So when they had dined, Jesus saith to Simon Peter, Simon, son of Jonas, lovest thou me more than these? He saith unto him, Yes, Lord; thou knowest that I love thee. He saith unto him, Feed my lambs.
16 He saith to him again the second time, Simon, son of Jonas, lovest thou me? He saith unto him, Yea, Lord; thou knowest that I love thee. He saith unto him, Feed my sheep.
17 He saith unto him the third time, Simon, son of Jonas, lovest thou me? Peter was grieved because he said unto him the third time, Lovest thou me? And he said unto him, Lord, thou knowest all things; thou knowest that I love thee. Jesus saith unto him, Feed my sheep.
18 Verily, verily, I say unto thee, When thou wast young, thou girdest thyself, and walkedst whither thou wouldest: but when thou shalt be old, thou shalt stretch forth thy hands, and another shall gird thee, and carry thee whither thou wouldest not.
19 This spake he, signifying by what death he should glorify God. And when he had spoken this, he saith unto him, Follow me.

That Jesus tells the disciples to go into Galilee – tells them either directly or through the women as messengers -- we have several witnesses. But the expedition to Galilee seems to lose track of itself somewhere along the way. Not everyone seems to have come along. And by the time the gospel narrative lets us in on it, the spiritual retreat seems to have been modified into a fishing trip!

The chronology is unclear. Any interpretation that hangs on an exact sequence for these last events in the four gospels is open to question. As in the later and present life of the church, the Lord is doing many different things at once –

at the same time as the church is doing several different things at once – things over which no one (not the ablest church leader) ever has control and of which none can even keep track! One of the things the church regularly does is wander – whether in the wilderness, amidst persecution, or in the midst of great works of God.

Jesus apparently met the disciples in the Upper Room twice – once when Thomas was missing and once when he was present. Apparently the "third time that Jesus showed himself to his disciples," (Luke 21:14) [gathered, for he'd showed himself to them singly and in pairs several other times], was at the sea of Tiberias (also known as the Sea of Galilee or the Sea of Kennereth.) Again, presumably 'showing himself to his disciples' here refers to the occasions when he showed himself to the <u>assembled</u> <u>church,</u> since we know he had already shown himself to Mary Magdalene, the other women, and the two on the Road to Emmaus. He foretells this third gathering, then directs them to go into Galilee to meet him at some particular mountain place (probably one of the mountains near the Sea of Galilee).

Despite this predicting, planning, and preparing, the gathering of disciples in Galilee seem to have lost focus. We can say this with some measure of confidence, because the appearance of the Lord comes as a surprise to them, something they (for the moment at least) are no longer expecting.

Seven of them have gone fishing as men tend to do when they need to "get away" and "get some peace and quiet". This is not just recreation, however, but it is (for at least four of them) their accustomed "work" – another activity into which "good men" escape. In addition, it seems that these men may have been prone to find escape another way: finding much comfort in familiar fellowship with each other, perhaps too much -- which I tentatively infer from Jesus' subsequent pointed questioning of Peter.

This setting and scene are reminiscent of much earlier scenes in the gospels. Peter and Andrew (he seems to be missing this time), James and John, were fishing when Jesus first met them – and called them. They abandoned their nets and their fathers' boats on those occasion. Now they seem to have come back to them.

But their fishing is fruitless. Their "peace and quiet" has become frustrating. Their "get away" has become 'the fish got away,' their hard work has "netted" them nothing, and perhaps their companionship has not proved as comforting as they hoped.

They hear a voice calling them. Again it is through hearing, the so-called "ear gate," that Jesus contacts them. Their eyes are once more little use to them – they do not recognize him. In the Upper Room he "appeared" among them, yet even there it was his words to them that gave them assurance and joy, as it was with the women and the two on the road to Emmaus. (Isn't it interesting that we speak of "calling" when we talk about the Lord's direction for our lives.) So often it is "appearances" of the Lord we long for, yet it is his words which get hold of us, his "voice" which transforms.

The stranger asks, "Children have you any meat?" Jesus begins as he begins many a conversation with us today -- 'Have you been able to provide for yourselves?' 'Have you found happiness in your own terms?' 'Is there peace and quiet now that you have been able to change your outward circumstances?' And if we answer honestly, we enter into a conversation that will bring grace and joy to replace our restlessness -- 'No, Lord – we haven't been able to produce one iota of satisfaction by ourselves.' On the other hand, we can go on pretending we have something to sustain us – maybe half of the sandwich we brought with us on the fishing trip. 'Oh, ya, we're doing just fine. Thanks for asking.' Where would the conversation have gone if that had been the disciples' response?

But they said 'no,' and the stranger's voice re-directs them. The trouble is, this stranger appears to be without authority, without expertise. After all, these guys are experienced fishermen. They know this business, this territory, this equipment. They know the weather, the season, the signs – and they know fish! How often we want to tell God to stick to his business and let us do ours! But they do as the voice of the stranger advises – one more time, perhaps just for the bare appearance of courtesy – and Wow! The nets come up full, nigh to bursting!

Again the Lord has condescended to reveal himself in terms men can understand. An abundance of fish where there were no fish indicates a supernatural factor. John is quick to comprehend, "It is the Lord." Peter, slower to 'get it,' is quickest to respond when he does – girding himself haphazardly, diving in, and swimming to shore.

And when they get to land, they find the stranger has a fire going – and bread and fish already prepared upon it. (Note that he has provided for them already – before their 'pay check' came in.) He tells them to haul in their nets and when they have seen with their eyes and counted the abundance, he says, "Come and Dine".

My wife and I for many years have enjoyed a forty year old recording by the Happy Goodman Family of a hundred year old song by Charles B. Widmeyer called "Come and Dine". One verse says:

The disciples came to land, thus obeying Christ's command
For the Master called to them, "Come and Dine"
There they found their heart's desire, bread and fish upon the fire,
Thus he satisfies the hungry all the time.

"Come and Dine," the Master calleth, "Come and dine."
You may feast at Jesus' table all the time
He who fed the multitudes, turned the water into wine
To the hungry calleth now, "Come and dine."

Jesus provides our heart's desire -- his abundance where we have nothing. It is where we are hungry that he provides food. The biblical theology of the song is quite extensive – the other verses connect the "come and dine" with the manna in the wilderness, and the wedding supper of the Lamb. As Jesus fed the multitudes in the wilderness, and broke bread with his disciples at the Last Supper – and as he was recognized by the two going to Emmaus in the breaking of the bread, so here in his provision the disciples all know who he is. He asked "Children, have you any meat?" They said no. He now replies in substance though two providing acts, 'Well I do.'

But this theme of feeding continues in the passage. As Thomas was on the 'hot seat' the second time in the upper room, now Peter is put under the uncomfortable light of Jesus' questioning. The question is repeated three times, which is an undeniable rebuke – even twice would have indicated some problem with Peter's answer. There are many nuances in the question and answers which I will not pursue here, but two things we cannot miss are the number and the feeding theme.

Jesus has already met Peter twice before. This is the third time! He has not confronted Peter or even made mild mention of Peter's denial of him up to now. Remember this bold Peter who swims to shore when he knows it is the Lord, is also he who boldly swore he would stick with Jesus through thick and thin – before Jesus' arrest. Yet after Jesus was arrested, Peter denied him three times – as Jesus predicted he would – on the same night he had vowed to go to the death with Jesus.

[I always find it powerful to think about Judas at this point – Judas and Peter. Two betrayers, two deniers, two men sorry for their cowardly and wrong actions. What was the difference between them? Was one better than the other? Was one rotten to the core and the other only slightly sinful? I don't think so. I think they were just the same – only one of them, by God's grace, repented and the other did not.]

Peter's impulsiveness, his tendency and ability to leap before he looks was not exclusive of the fear of man. (Often we mistake boldness in men as moral courage, when in fact it is only a reflex or even a defensive tactic.) Peter's motive in denying Jesus was simply that – the fear of man. Jesus begins his questioning of Peter by asking, "Simon, son of Jonas, do you love me more than these?" 'Do you love me more than men?' 'Is your love for me such that all other loves, desires for respect, and fears of reprisal are secondary?' This is the Lord's way – to go right to the heart of our sin.

Jesus is not only "bringing up" Peter's sin. He is offering a direct opportunity for Peter to acknowledge it and repent. The three repetitions are confirming to Peter that his denials are history. The three affirmations are the final blows which knock each of the three denials in the head. This isn't penance, it isn't atonement for his own sins, but it is a sacramental profession – a memorial and seal. Sometimes when we have sinned seriously we need a ceremony, a deliberate memorial ritual, to re-affirm our faith – before God, before others, and as a milestone for our own re-orientation.

"Feed my sheep" and "feed my lambs". The fullest and most abiding description of the work of a church leader – indeed of the church. (Indeed, the three words, "shepherd," "flock," and "feed" have the same Greek root.)

The great commission follows – defines the "whom," the church. But here Peter is told (and so are we) what we are to do – to feed the lambs, to feed the sheep. Growing up among a few of them in Montana, I have seen how much work this activity takes on the part of a rancher or shepherd. Few things are more hum-drum, more time-consuming, and nothing ties a man down more than feeding flocks and herds. The desire to do something more exciting and dynamic is strong in us all. But the church really hasn't anything "more" to do. The lambs and sheep need to brought in, it is true. Sometimes they need to be found in the far thickets where they are lost. But the central job description is feeding them. We are to pass on the message, "Come and Dine!" We are to offer the bread and fish Jesus has given us – to those other empty-handed fishermen around us.

And we are to feed them steadily, repeatedly (another aspect of the three repetitions). The sheep and the lambs – the old and the young, in years and in the faith. Feed my sheep.

But see the three-point transition. 'Peter , love me more than your best friends.' And when Peter affirms that his affections, his love are centered firmly on Jesus, then Jesus calls him to re-direct his heart again – 'feed my sheep'. Our love must continually move from the world to Jesus, and then, out of love for Jesus, our love must focus in our neighbor. As in the verses at the end of I John 4 and the beginning of I John 5, there is a divine dynamic, a movement back and forth of our consciousness between the love of God and the love of man, which cannot become static (merely formal) on either hand without losing its essence. (That may be a poor metaphor, but look at the I John passages for the essence of what I'm after.)

Jesus' last word to Peter here (about eventually being "girded" and led by others) is often discussed as a particular prophesy of Peter's own martyrdom, but it has a simpler level, too – a reminder of mortality. 'Feed my sheep, but remember you will die.' Mortality is the immovable monument to our weakness, but also to the term of our calling. 'Feed my sheep aware at all times of your limits', but also, 'Feed my sheep – until I call you home to your rest.' And, inescapably, Peter must have heard that difficult mercy of God here, too. As Thomas's words became the definition of how he would affirm his faith in Christ, so Peter's brave words at the Last Supper are to ultimately be fulfilled – he will follow Jesus to death – he will die with Jesus.

As the explication at the end of the passage implies, the prophecy also implies, 'Feed my sheep until the wolves get you, and thus I relieve you of your duties.'

Chapter Twelve: Real End, Real Beginning

– The Ascension

Matthew 28:18-20
18 And Jesus came and spake unto them, saying, All power is given unto me in heaven and earth.
19 Go ye therefore, and teach all nations, baptizing them in the name of the Father, and of the Son, and of the Holy Ghost:
20 Teaching them to observe all things whatsoever I have commanded you: and lo, I am with you always, even unto the end of the world. Amen.

Mark 16:19-20
19 So then after the Lord had spoken unto them, he was received up into heaven, and sat on the right hand of God.
20 And they went forth, and preached every where, the Lord working with them, and confirming the word with signs following. Amen.

(see also Mark 16: 15-18)

Luke 24: 48-53
48 And ye are witnesses of these things.
49 And behold, I send the promise of my Father upon you: but tarry ye in the city of Jerusalem, until ye be endued with power from on high.
50 And he led them out as far as to Bethany, and he lifted up his hands, and blessed them.
51 And it came to pass, while he blessed them, he was parted from them, and carried up into heaven.
52 And they worshiped him, and returned to Jerusalem with great joy:
53 And were continually in the temple, praising and blessing God. Amen.

Acts 1:1-14
1 The former treatise have I made, O Theophilus, of all that Jesus began to do and teach,
2 Until the day in which he was taken up, after that he through the Holy Ghost had given commandments unto the apostles whom he had chosen:

3 To whom also he showed himself alive after his passion by many infallible proofs, being seen of them forty days, and speaking of the things pertaining to the kingdom of God:

4 And being assembled together with them, commanded them that they should not depart from Jerusalem, but wait for the promise of the Father, which, saith he, ye have heard of me.

5 For John truly baptized with water; but ye shall be baptized with the Holy Ghost not many days hence.

6 When they therefore were come together, they asked of him, saying, Lord wilt thou at this time restore again the kingdom to Israel?

7 And he said unto them, It is not for you to know the times or the seasons which the Father hath put in his own power.

8 But ye shall receive power, after that the Holy Ghost is come upon you: and ye shall be witnesses unto me both in Jerusalem, and in all Judea, and in Samaria, and unto the uttermost parts of the earth.

9 And when he had spoken these things, while they beheld, he was taken up; and a cloud received him out of their sight.

10 And while they looked steadfastly toward heaven as he went up, behold, two men stood by them in white apparel;

11 Which also said, Ye men of Galilee, why stand ye gazing up into heaven? This same Jesus, which is taken up from you into heaven, shall come in like manner as ye have seen him go into heaven.

12 Then returned they unto Jerusalem from the mount called Olivet, which is from Jerusalem a sabbath day's journey.

13 And when they were come in, they went up into an upper room, where abode both Peter and James, and John, and Andrew, Philip, and Thomas, Bartholomew, and Matthew, James the son of Alphaeus, and Simon Zelotes, and Judas, the brother of James.

14. These all continued with one accord in prayer and supplication, with the women, and Mary the mother of Jesus, and with his brethren.

Last words are important. Books have been published consisting exclusively of the final few sentences to come from mortal mouths. However, the four gospel-writers seem to be motivated by something more than adulation of the dearest-departed. For them this is not about final words – it is about introductory words – the preface to the age of the church and the Age of the Spirit.

The great commission has been extensively discussed by many students wiser than I. I only touch on its points here as the Lord spoke them:

- All power on heaven and earth is given to me (Jesus)

  - Ye (my disciples/people) shall receive power after the Holy Ghost is come upon you

    - {Go back to Jerusalem and wait until ye be endued with power from on high – until you are baptized with the Holy Spirit as I previously said you would be}

- Go THEREFORE and teach all nations.

  - Ye shall be witnesses to me in Jerusalem and in all Judea, and in Samaria, and unto the uttermost parts of the earth.
  - Baptize them in the name of the Father and the Son and the Holy Ghost,
  - Teaching them to observe all things whatsoever I have commanded you.

- Lo, I am with you always, even unto the end of the age.

The Lord ascends into heaven before the gathered church. The witnesses of this crowning event, this final event of his earthly ministry, are exclusively the apostles. There are no centurions, no curious crowds, no guardian soldiers as there were for the death and resurrection. It is given to the church alone to see this last glorious act of the Lord – they are ready to be his witnesses, they are trusted to be the sole testifiers of his ascent into heaven. Indeed, when the promised Holy Spirit does come, they are made witnesses of what their eyes cannot have seen (or not at least until Paul and John were given the visions they mention in the New Testament) – that

Jesus not only ascended into the clouds, but into heaven, where he sat down at God the Father's right hand.

These slow-learners (always so obviously our spiritual grandfathers) are still in the dark about many things. They still ask (if not dumb, then immature) questions: 'Lord, are you going to restore the kingdom <u>now</u>?' One can almost hear the childish rising lilt in that final word – like the advertising slogan spoken by the child traveling with its parents, 'Are we there <u>yet</u>?' But Jesus does not speak to them as to children – or at least now it is more as though he were speaking to maturing adolescents, "It is not for you to know the times or the seasons which the Father hath put in his own power." Not a rebuke, but a statement of principle to be remembered.

And when he ascends, they stand around craning their necks toward the sky – how long would they have stayed there! But angels, "two men . . . in white apparel", speak the last mild rebuke found in the gospels, reminiscent of the angels speaking to Mary Magdalene at the tomb. "Ye men of Galilee, why stand ye gazing up into heaven?" And also as with Mary, it is more than a mild rebuke, it is a final affirmation of the ultimate end, the final promise, "This same Jesus, which is taken up from you into heaven, shall come in like manner as ye have seen him go into heaven."

In contrast to their "yet dark" state between the crucifixion and the revelation of the resurrection, they are left with an incredible amount of "data," an abundance of light -- what is elsewhere called an "exceeding and eternal weight of glory"(II Corinthians 4:17-18). As much as remains mysterious and unknown, they do not seem to feel at all "in the dark" at this point. They know what they are to do (to wait); and where (in Jerusalem); they know what is to happen to them in the immediate future (power is to come upon them, the promised Holy Spirit); they know what they are to do beyond that, and for the rest of their lives (go, teach, baptize, disciple); and where (in Jerusalem, all of Judaea, Samaria, and to the uttermost parts of the earth); they know that some of them are to die for their faith (the prophesy to Peter); they know that

Jesus will ultimately return as he came; and they know that in another but certain sense he will be "with them" until the end (the Spirit will be their Comforter and reminder). But most amazing of all, they are ready to receive this light! Their faith has been made such that they can receive what otherwise would be useless, 'indigestible' or 'incomprehensible' data to them.

Thus it is in our lives when things are, when <u>we</u> are in the dark. The first thing God does is to make our faith such that it can receive light – to fill our lamps with oil, or to make our eye "single," 'transparent'. Then he will give us as much "light" as we can handle. Our flesh demands the opposite order – 'Lord, show me, then I'll believe!' Gently, but firmly, the Lord turns our world and our thinking upside down – until we can believe and <u>then</u> see aright.

I have indicated I am of the conviction that the coming of the Holy Ghost predicted here is on the literal level a strict reference to Pentecost and to the several reverberations of that event out into the world (in the second circle – Peter's vision and Cornelius – Acts 10:1-11:18; in the third circle – Paul's bringing of the Holy Spirit to the Gentile lands – Acts 13:1-19:7). There are nevertheless a number of wider applications by way of analogy to the Lord's injunction to return to Jerusalem and wait.

On one level, it is certain although paradoxical that many of the Lord's commissions which involve us going or doing begin with commands to wait. This would seem to be saying the opposite of what we saw with Mary Magdalene – that the Lord tells her to get doing before she can embrace him – work before resting. But waiting and resting are not the same thing. Waiting, in fact, is often the hardest kind of work. It is a poised posture, the stance of the runner in the starting blocks, or the pregnant woman in the stirrups, or the patient in the dentist's waiting room. Notice where the disciples gather and what they end up doing there.

They gather in the upper room (again – an incredibly important spot – if there was ever a place for a shrine that would be it) and they end up praying – "with one accord in prayer and supplication" – that messiest and most hard to define, yet certainly commanded activity of the church. My wife is a pray-er. I think it is only honest to say I am not. We argue about the place of prayer. I am inclined to call her a pietist. Yet when all is said and done and others of us have worn out our activist instincts – it is to prayer we (even I) go. And not just any prayer, either. The prayer of the upper room is of one accord and it is "supplication," which is only a polite word for begging.

They also were "continually" in the Temple – praising and blessing God. Worshipping continually is the way to maintain a "waiting" stance before the Lord. We are attentive when we worship – focused on the one being who is important – like the runner focused on the starter, the pregnant woman focused on the baby, and the patient focused on the one who will call him from the waiting room into the surgery.

But the temple is no longer a building (a pet peeve of mine!). The continual praise and blessing of God takes place in the midst of the church, which is exclusively people – a shrine made of living stones, not inanimate ones! If buildings are to be thought of, let us think first of our homes for indeed we see that is where the church gathers at the Lord's command here, and on into the first chapters of Acts. It is in the homes they gather for teaching and eating. It is in the homes that they continue in fellowship. Yet these buildings are not especially "sacred," either, for they do not hesitate to sell them in order to provide for each others needs. (Acts 2)

Prayer is what the church does as it waits for things to be made clear – and as it waits for power from God. There is such a thing as a pietist error – substituting prayer or the motions of worship for going and doing, just as there is such a thing as a quietist error – lacking the intentionality which goes with faith, but neither of these is the central concern of the church as it waits for God's appointment. The American church does, at strange moments, substitute prayer for obedience in other ways, but much more often our sin is in the opposite direction – too little prayer, too much running around like headless chickens.

And although we can say Pentecost has come once and for all in history just as the crucifixion and resurrection have come once and for all, yet there is still a need for each of us to repeat this pattern of waiting for power and light in our lives. Through the Holy Spirit we must apprehend the Lord's work for each of us and for us together (what have been called the existential facets of faith), and to wait on the Lord to empower us (an overused but accurate phrase insofar as its denotation goes). Furthermore, there is a sense in which this pattern must be repeated each time we set out on the Lord's commission – at the beginning of each phase of our calling, each day, each hour, indeed, each moment!

Jesus blesses the church as he bids them to wait. They go away to "wait" rejoicing. They continually praise and bless God, as they worship in the Temple and as they gather to pray with one accord in the upper room. Waiting for Jesus is not like waiting in the dentist's office for our appointment – it is not supposed to be an expectation of something painful, fearful. We are not meant to be stoic, or even merely patient. If we know him who has told us to wait, we know we are blessed, we rejoice, we bless him in return. That is a long way from my usual attitude! Lord, give me a heart to wait joyfully. If the apostles, having not yet received the fullness of the Spirit could continually rejoice, what excuse have I!

In the introduction and transition to the Book of Acts, we are told that the disciples did indeed go into all the world preaching and teaching, the Lord confirming their work with signs following. The immediate promises were fulfilled as Jesus had said they would be.

Finally, for these meditations, I find a warm "kiss" of God in the closing verse of the last passage here (introductory section of the first chapter of Acts.) Just as Jesus took time on the cross to commend Mary, his mother, and John to one another – a wonderful affirmation of his "human" love as well as his divine love, so here we see that Jesus' family – his mother and brothers are gathered with his "spiritual" children, the apostles. To me this is yet another declaration that Christ's love is organic, that the church is meant to be families and a family as well as something bigger – and that we are not to discount our organic relationships in the name of something "higher" or "bigger" or "more efficient".

It is true that in extremity a family may sometimes have to close its doors against one of its members – until certain conditions of repentance or at least reform are met. Likewise the church. (We neither hasten to do this nor fail to hope and pray it will be but for a brief time.) But the church can never dismiss a concern for its members in the name of expediency or goals or a "vision," any more than a family can. Nobody had or will have more important business than Jesus himself. Nobody ever had or will have greater need for efficiency than Jesus had. But he who was careful to make it clear that his mother and brothers in the flesh had no higher priority than other women and men, makes a point of caring for his own family at the cross. And here we see that his family according to the flesh is part of his family according to the Spirit – that the covenants and promises are not meant to be dichotomized.

Conclusion :

When it's Dark for You and for Me

All of God's people have experienced a good deal of darkness, beginning with Adam and Eve hiding in the woods, and then cast out of the beautiful garden into a world darkened by their sin. Noah and Abraham were often in the dark during years of confusion. Isaac unsure of his father's sacrifice, Joseph betrayed by his brothers and in Pharaoh's prison, Moses as half-prince in Egypt, then before the burning bush, and Israel over and over in the wilderness and in the Promised Land – dark episode after dark episode.

In one sense we are all in the dark all of the time during our sojourn in this world. Great saints have majored on this topic – and their point is not in error, unless it be made exclusive of the opposite fact – that into our darkness has shown a great light (Isaiah 60; John 1). We see as in a mirror dimly – but we shall see face to face. Moreover we live in both this present and this future. The Holy Spirit has been given to us, bringing all things to the minds of the Bible writers, and witnessing with our spirits to the truth of their words, God's word. We are in process – learning, growing, being convicted of sin, of righteousness and of judgment to come. We are being changed from one degree of glory into the next and being conformed to the image of the Son. And when we see him face to face <u>we</u> <u>shall</u> <u>be</u> <u>like</u> <u>him</u>!

But now all our knowledge is analogous. It is true knowledge, yet it is not knowledge as God knows. We do not know immediately (that is without intermediary means). We only know in images and pictures and formulas and words. We are in a certain sense still very much in the dark.

85.

Moreover at many places in our lives we are particularly in the dark – not even knowing by analogy, but rather having an acute sense of our unknowing – often a painful and even agonizing sense of being clueless. At these points, we are like Mary Magdalene, Thomas, Peter, and yes, Judas. May God give us grace to return to his Word, and perhaps particularly to these passages where we see the church in the extremity of crisis, stumbling about, "while it was yet dark." May the Holy Spirit, the Spirit which raised Christ from the dead, keep us in a path of faith dimly as we may perceive it. May we be held up by that mysterious and inexplicable grace which makes for persistence and courage when no earthly reason may be summoned to support them. May we "keep on keeping on" until the dawn breaks again, until the last stone rolls away, until the Lord speaks our name. As he will.

Meanwhile, although it is yet dark, it is he by his grace and in the power of his Holy Spirit who keeps us. It is not our own understandings anymore than our own righteousness. It is our glorious Lord, himself.

God Moves in a Mysterious Way
William Cowper, 1774

[Published in *Twenty-six Letters on Religious Subjects,* by John Newton, 1774. It is said to be the last hymn Cowper wrote, with several versions of the story behind it coming down to us. Common to all versions, however, is Cowper's struggle with depression and doubt, in the midst of which he was close to self-destruction, at which time God delivered him through remarkable circumstances.]

God moves in a mysterious way
His wonders to perform;
He plants His footsteps in the sea
And rides upon the storm.
Deep in unfathomable mines
Of never failing skill
He treasures up His bright designs
And works His sov'reign will.
Ye fearful saints, fresh courage take;
The clouds ye so much dread
Are big with mercy and shall break
In blessings on your head.
Judge not the Lord by feeble sense,
But trust Him for His grace;
Behind a frowning providence
He hides a smiling face.
His purposes will ripen fast,
Unfolding every hour;
The bud may have a bitter taste,
But sweet will be the flow'r.
Blind unbelief is sure to err
And scan His work in vain;
God is His own interpreter,
And He will make it plain.

Psalms 30
Thanksgiving for Deliverance from Death
A Psalm and Song at the dedication of the house of David.

I will extol thee, O Lord ; for thou hast lifted me up,
and hast not made my foes to rejoice over me.
O Lord my God, I cried unto thee,
and thou hast healed me.
O Lord, thou hast brought up my soul from the grave :
thou hast kept me alive,
that I should not go down to the pit.
Sing unto the Lord, O ye saints of his, and give thanks
at the remembrance of his holiness.
For his anger endureth but a moment ;
in his favor is life :
weeping may endure for a night, but joy cometh in the
morning.
And in my prosperity I said, I shall never be moved.
Lord, by thy favor thou hast made my mountain to
stand strong : thou didst hide thy face,
and I was troubled.
I cried to thee, O Lord; and unto the Lord I made
supplication.
What profit is there in my blood,
when I go down to the pit ?
Shall the dust praise thee ? Shall it declare thy truth ?
Hear, O Lord, and have mercy upon me :
Lord, be thou my helper.
Thou hast turned for me my mourning into dancing :
thou hast put off my sackcloth,
and girded me with gladness ;
to the end that my glory may sing praise to thee,
and not be silent.
O Lord my God, I will give thanks unto thee for ever.